SECRET
EALING

Paul Howard Lang and
Dr Jonathan Oates

AMBERLEY

This book is dedicated to Julia Tubman and her staff at Gunnersbury Park Museum

First published 2020

Amberley Publishing
The Hill, Stroud
Gloucestershire, GL5 4EP

www.amberley-books.com

Copyright © Paul Howard Lang and
Dr Jonathan Oates, 2020

The right of Paul Howard Lang and Dr Jonathan Oates
to be identified as the Authors of this work has been
asserted in accordance with the Copyrights, Designs
and Patents Act 1988.

ISBN 978 1 4456 9567 9 (print)
ISBN 978 1 4456 9568 6 (ebook)

British Library Cataloguing in Publication Data.
A catalogue record for this book is available from the
British Library.

Typesetting by Aura Technology and Software
Services, India. Printed in Great Britain.

Contents

Introduction

There have been many books published about the histories of Ealing, Acton, Southall and the other constituent districts which now form the London Borough of Ealing, from the late nineteenth century onwards. This book is not a historical narrative, as many are, nor is it a collection of pictures with captions. Instead it is a number of stories taken from the histories of these localities, which are generally unknown or little known at present. Hence the title 'Secret' Ealing. The ideal reader is envisaged as one who has a general knowledge of Ealing's historical development, but is wanting to know more about some of the more obscure aspects of that history.

It may be worth outlining a very brief account of Ealing's history, assuming that term is not a misnomer. In fact, for much of that history it is best to think of the histories of seven settlements: Acton, Ealing, Greenford, Hanwell, Northolt, Perivale and Southall/Norwood. All these were small villages in the county of Middlesex, a county that was mostly rural

Ealing.

Fifty years ago Ealing was little more than a rural village. Situated about 6½ miles from London on the G.W. main line from Paddington, its popularity as a residential neighbourhood, is rapidly increasing. The Public Buildings, Churches, and fine shops clearly show its prosperity. The main street —The Broadway, stands on the Oxford Road, in which are most of the principal public buildings, and business establishments, among these may be mentioned the Town Hall, and Hippodrome, the latter of recent date, and one of the most complete suburban houses of amusement.

It is particularly rich in parks and open spaces, comprising in all about 117 acres, mostly under the control of the Town Council. Here during the summer months the Town Band gives frequent Open-Air Concerts while ample facilities are afforded for various outdoor sports and every kind of recreation.

Two excellent Golf Courses are also in the borough.

The town stands fairly high, upon a subsoil of gravel in which have been found bones and teeth of the hippopotamus, the elephant, and the bullock. The Church, dedicated to St. Mary, was erected in 1735, it is a brick building with square tower and copula. Christ Church, St. John's, St. Peter's are all of more recent date.

One of the most interesting places in this district is the quaint old church of Perivale, said to have been erected prior to the Conquest. The chancel and nave are either brick or stone, entirely covered with plaster, while the little tower is surmounted by a cap of wood; let in the wood work are two or three little windows, a sundial occupying a place about half way up, the whole presenting a most pleasing and interesting picture.

Ealing, c. 1910.

until the nineteenth century, yet also contained the metropolis of the British Empire and the capital city of Great Britain. Each of these places had its own history, but generally speaking were all farming communities with small populations and which included a church, a number of mansions and landed estates. Some were interlinked by the main road running west from London to Oxford, and later, by the Great Western Railway. Each administered itself, with supervision at county level.

It was only in the late nineteenth century that these places began to resemble towns, with all the amenities that were needed as populations rose. Farmland and open land began to disappear as many streets of housing were built on them. Trams and buses plied the roads, underground trains supplemented the Great Western trains. Public services grew as secular councils replaced parish vestries. Industries were established in Acton and Southall. By 1914, Hanwell, Acton, Southall and Ealing were all substantial towns and housing was beginning to merge together, so it was becoming difficult to tell where one parish began and another ended. In the 1900s Ealing adopted the nom de plume 'Queen of the Suburbs'.

In the 1920s and 1930s the once rural Greenford and Perivale were increasingly suburban as private houses and industries replaced farmland and cottages. By now districts were beginning to merge together, not just as regards the suburban sprawl, but administratively. Hanwell, Greenford, Perivale, Northolt and Ealing merged to become the Borough of Ealing in 1926–28. Aerial bombing was deadly in 1940–44, but far less so than elsewhere in Greater London. After the war, Northolt was built over and its once famous

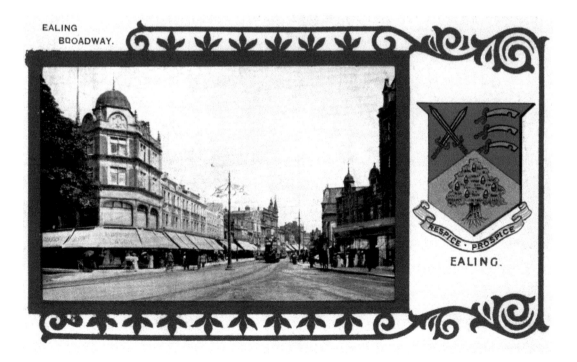

Ealing Broadway.

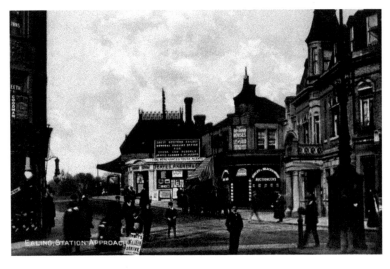

Left: Station Approach, Ealing.

Below: Ealing.

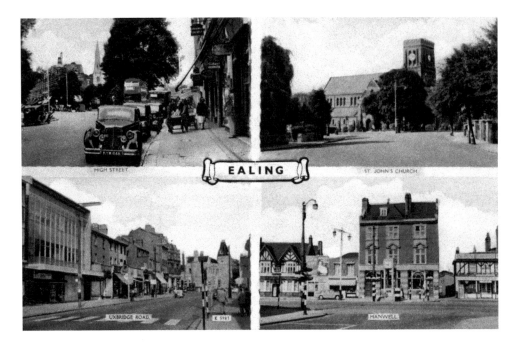

racecourse was now no more. In 1965 the London Borough of Ealing was established as a result of the merger of the three boroughs of Acton, Ealing and Southall.

Readers needing more detail should consult histories of individual districts; those by the author include *Acton: A History* (2003) *Southall and Hanwell History and Guide* (2003), and E*aling: A Concise History* (2014), and Frances Hounsell's *Greenford, Northolt and Perivale Past* (1999). Most of the information in this book concerns aspects of local history hitherto little explored. They include espionage, crime, controversies, vanished buildings, most of which do not feature in these works.

1. Ancient and Medieval Ealing

If you walk around Ealing you will see much evidence of the twenty-first and twentieth centuries as well as quite a lot of the nineteenth century all around you in the sense of not only buildings, but infrastructure, open spaces, transport and of course, people. Local history goes back centuries before the birth of Christ and the arrival of the Romans, but there is very little evidence of it in both terms of written documentation, physical remains or buildings. There are no ruined abbeys, monasteries or castles to denote obvious antiquity.

Yet we can learn about the borough's ancient and medieval past. Easiest to see are those buildings which survive. Usually the oldest buildings are the ancient parish churches, in each of the seven settlements that now form the borough. However, population growth in the nineteenth century led to most of these churches being rebuilt and so are mostly Victorian in structure.

Three do survive, admittedly altered over the centuries. These are in the north of the modern borough: St Mary the Virgin Perivale, just south of the A40 (a now redundant church but a lively arts venue); St Mary's Northolt; and the old Holy Trinity church in Greenford, overshadowed by its 1941 successor. Fortunately, none of these places expanded their population substantially in the nineteenth century and when the population explosions occurred in the 1930s, there was the knowledge that old buildings of merit were worthy of preservation.

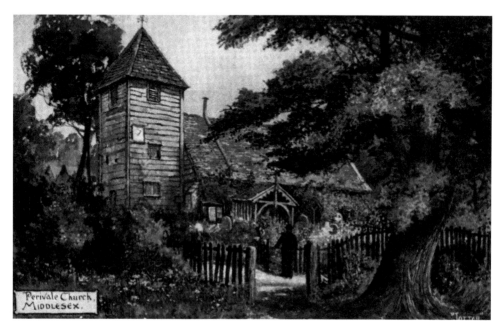

Perivale Church, external view.

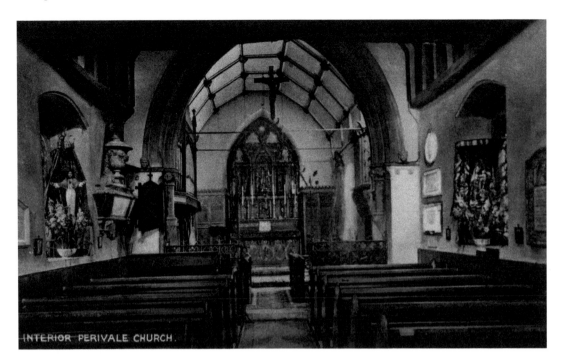

Perivale Church, interior view.

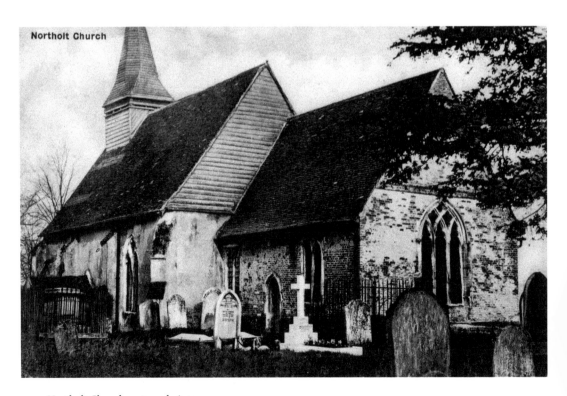

Northolt Church, external view.

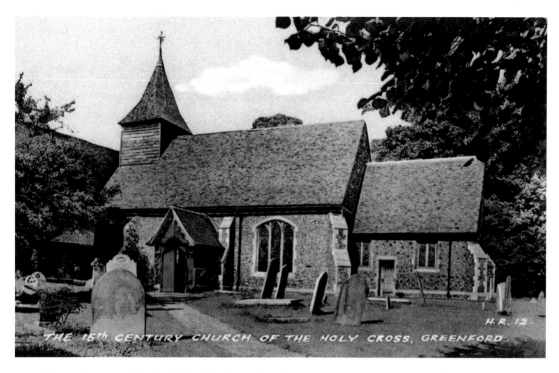

THE 15th CENTURY CHURCH OF THE HOLY CROSS, GREENFORD.

Fifteenth-century Church of the Holy Cross, Greenford.

All three date from the twelfth century, though much of the existing fabric dates from the thirteenth and more, the fourteenth centuries.

The interiors of these churches also merit investigation for all include brasses of a few of the locality's medieval residents. At St Mary's Perivale can be seen the Myllet family (whom Perivale's first pub was to be named after) – father, two wives and a dozen children. At St Mary's Church in Ealing is a brass of Richard Amondesham, a landowner and merchant of fifteenth- century Ealing. The inscription reads, 'Here under lyeth Richard Amondesham, otherwise called Awnsham, some tyme mercer and marnchaunt of the staple of Calys, and Kateryn, his wyff, on whose soules Jesus have mercy'. The font at Northolt and the piscina (a basin near the altar to wash communion vessels) at Greenford date from the fourteenth century.

There are traces remaining of Northolt manor house, overlooking the church. These were subject to excavations in the 1950s and 1960s which involved Charles Keene, an amateur Northolt historian. The manor house had been destroyed in a fire in the late fourteenth century and never rebuilt. Yet the excavation was significant because it gave an outline of a medieval manor house. The Le Boteler family built a stone manor house here in 1231 and it was at its peak of prosperity in the following century when Simon Francis, a City merchant and Sheriff, the new lord, had it rebuilt in 1346.

It was now far larger than before, with a great hall and living quarters, known as solars, above it. There was decorative brickwork and white patterned tiles from Penn in Buckinghamshire. There was a moat around the house. There were cellars, kitchens and outhouses within a

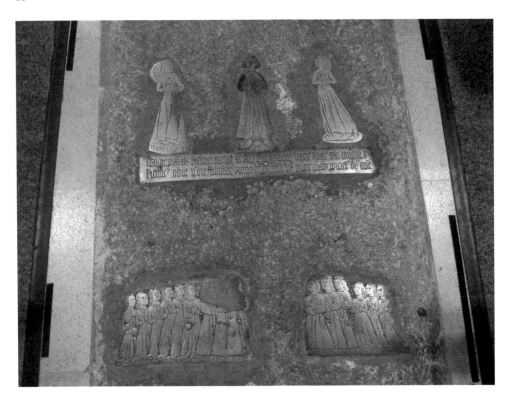

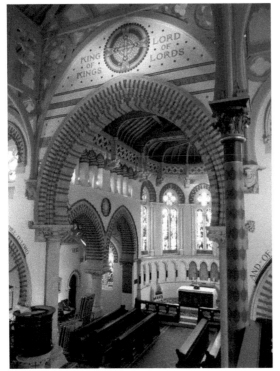

Above: Myllet brass in Perivale Church, *c.* 1500.

Left: Interior view from the gallery of St Mary's Church, Ealing.

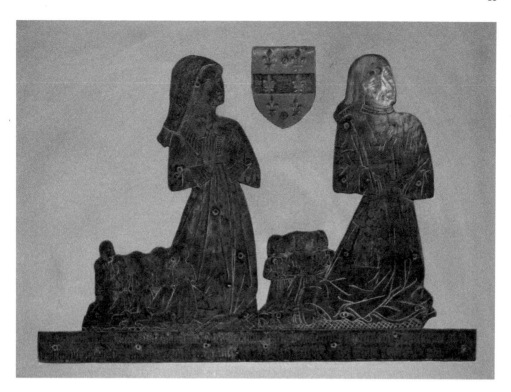

Amondesham brass in St Mary's Church, Ealing.

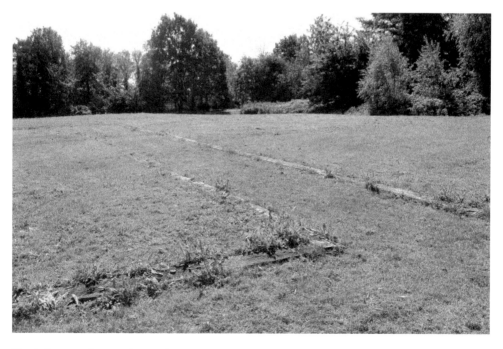

Northolt moated manor house site.

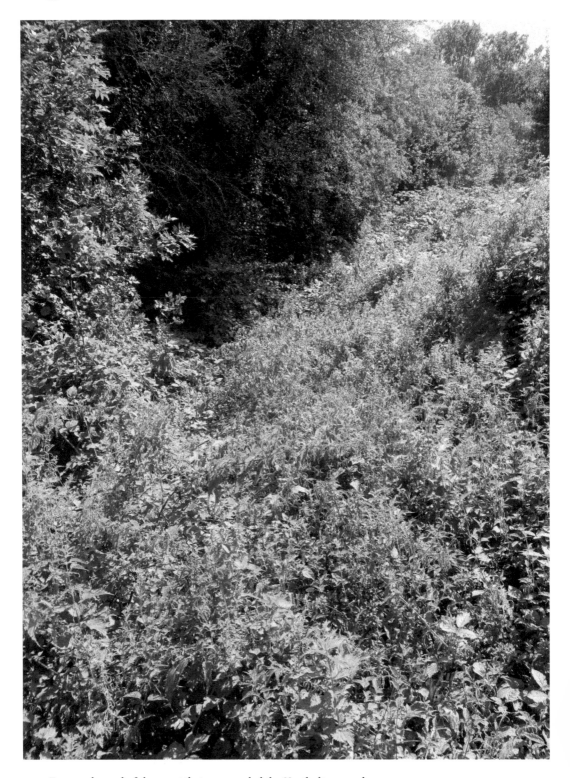

Former channel of the moat that surrounded the Northolt manor house.

13

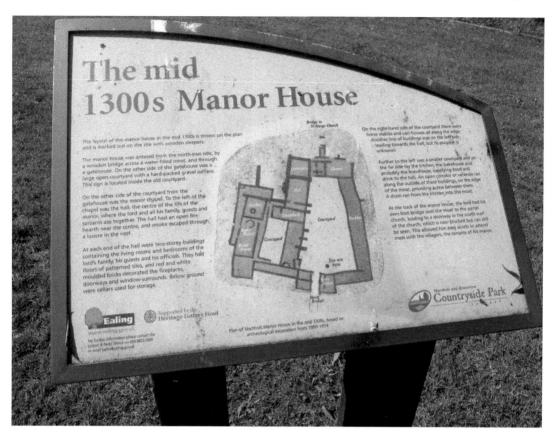

Information board on the Northolt moated manor house site.

walled enclosure. Alice Turner later inherited it and had it partly demolished in 1370. There was rebuilding again by Nicholas Brembre, a new owner, in 1372, but it did not last long and following his execution for treason in 1388 it was again knocked down. The site remains and there are explanatory boards there.

Older even than human existence were the beasts of the Pleistocene period, between 25,000 and 50,000 years ago. Mammoth remains were found during the excavations for the Southall Gas Works in the 1870s.

DID YOU KNOW?

A woolly mammoth bone was found during excavations at Tentelow Lane, Norwood Green, in 1887. Portions of bone and tooth were found under Kingsley Avenue in Southall in June 1942. It is supposed that at this time the district lay on the banks of the Thames and formed marshland, ideal for such hunting.

There is abundant archaeological evidence for the presence of prehistoric peoples in Ealing, as we have so much in the way of lithic artefacts. Flints have been found in the vicinity of The Grove, Grange Road and Beaconsfield Road in Ealing, also in Hanwell and on the former Southall Gas Works site. Also the remains of Stone Age pottery have been found under Ealing Common. A great many flint axe heads, dating from 400,000 to 200,000 years old, are the oldest evidence of human activity in Acton.

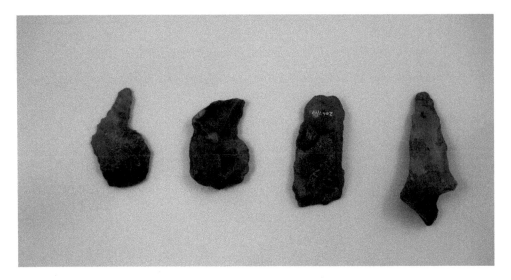

Hanwell, Palaeolithic scrapers, Sadler Bequest 1. (Gunnersbury Park Museum)

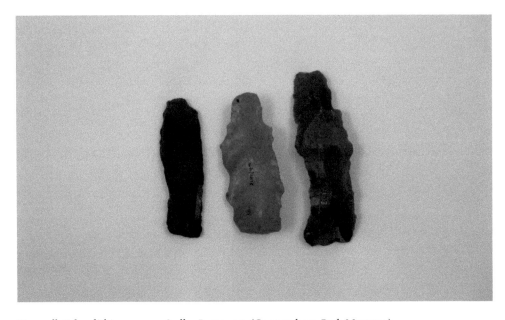

Hanwell, Palaeolithic scrapers, Sadler Bequest 2. (Gunnersbury Park Museum)

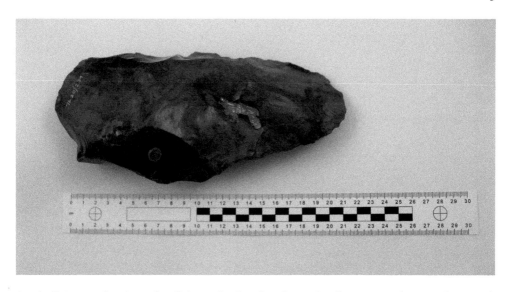

Southall Gas Works site, Palaeolithic Acheulian hand axe, Crooke Bequest. (Gunnersbury Park Museum)

Sharp flint spearheads and other weapons and tools were also found under what became Creffield Road in Acton, leading an early twentieth-century commentator to anachronistically suggest that this was the origin of Acton's then industrial predominance. There is also evidence for Neolithic burials near Mill Hill Park. Further to this there are also the Southall palstave axes and axe mould found in a field in the nineteenth century

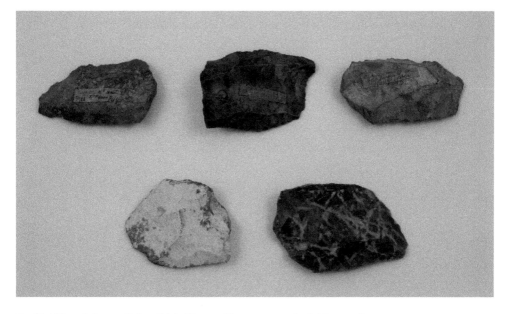

Creffield Road, Acton, Palaeolithic flints 1. (Gunnersbury Park Museum)

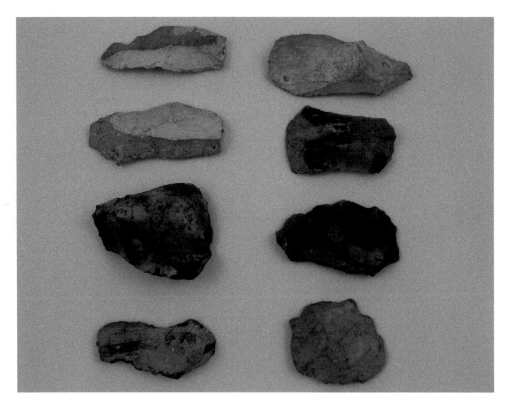

Creffield Road, Acton, Palaeolithic flints 2. (Gunnersbury Park Museum)

which date to the Bronze Age and are a rare and important find. An axe mould may indicate that metalworking was going on locally at this time. Iron Age coins have been found near Bollo Lane.

The Romans left very little mark on this district. Six Romano-British funeral urns, made of Samian ware, and a rare gold coin of Macedonian origin, all dating from the second century AD, have been found in north Ealing. This is possibly evidence of a temporary and small settlement to the west of Londinium. Roman coins and pottery have also been found in what was Hanwell Park and on Boston Lane. On Acton Green have been found some Roman pottery and coins, together with a lamp and tile from the Sixth Legion. These may be connected to the fact that there was a Roman road just to the south of our district.

Saxon remains have been found under the land where Oakland's Road School in southern Hanwell was built. These were the remains of ten fifth- or sixth-century Saxon warriors. Fifty spearheads were found nearby. This has led Sir Montagu Sharpe, a local historian, to state that there was fighting – 'The Battle of Bloody Croft' – in Hanwell, but there is no evidence as to how these Saxons died, so this is mere wishful speculation. Saxon brooches of gilt and bronze have also been found in Hanwell and at nearby Dormers Wells was Saxon pottery. A Saxon sword called a seax has been found at Northolt, dating from the seventh century. Also Saxon graves were found beneath the Northolt manor house site.

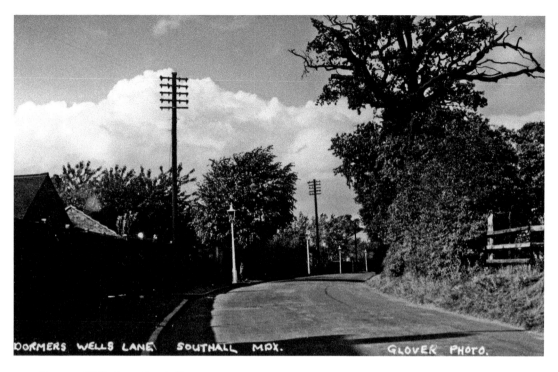

Dormers Wells Lane, Southall.

It is almost certain, therefore, together with the existence of charters conveying land in both Norwood and Ealing that this district was settled by the Saxons at the latest. Churches and manor were probably also established then, but apart from that there is very little else that can be stated with any certainty as the evidence is so limited.

This district was partially covered by the great Norman Domesday survey of 1086, but regrettably Ealing and Acton, being part of the manor of Fulham, were not recorded separately and Norwood being part of the manor of Hayes was also not recorded individually. Hanwell and Northolt were recorded individually as manors in Middlesex, and the concise information recorded therein gives an insight into society at the time.

The lord of the manor of Hanwell was the Abbot of Westminster Abbey. During the reign of Edward the Confessor, the manor yielded an annual income of £7, but a quarter century on, it had dropped to £5 10 shillings. Just over half of the agricultural land in the manor was owned by the lord and it came with one plough. The other land was farmed by four ploughs belonging to the villeins, or peasants, who farmed four hides (a hide being 120 acres). One villein held two hides, the remainder held one between them and six bordars (ranking below a villein, but above a serf in the medieval hierarchy) farmed the remainder. There were also people who did not hold land: four cottagers and lowest of the low, two serfs. There was also a mill, a wood sufficient for fifty pigs and meadowland enough for a plough team. This suggests a community of seventeen householders, so assuming average family size of five, then Hanwell had around eighty-five residents at this time.

Greenford had the same lord of the manor as Hanwell, but at eleven and a half hides was a little larger. Population was greater, too; there were nine villeins, seven bordars, three cottagers, six slaves and a Frenchman. There was far more woodland, enough to support 300 pigs. However, there may have been two sub manors: one being held by Geoffrey de Mandeville, with two villeins, two cottagers and a slave; and another being held by Aelfeva directly from the King, which was a mere half hide. This may have been Perivale or Greenford Parva.

Northolt was a large manor, too, with fifteen hides and was held by Geoffrey de Mandeville. There were seventeen villeins, three cottagers, six slaves and, uniquely for these three manors, one priest, suggesting a church at Northolt by the late eleventh century.

Documentation for these medieval manors, in terms of manorial court rolls, can be found at the London Metropolitan Archives for most of these manors except for Northolt and that is to be found at Westminster Abbey Archives. The Victoria County History for Middlesex volumes 3–4 and 7 gives additional details and references to these documents, but no comprehensive history of medieval Ealing has ever been compiled.

2. Controversies

In the decades between the World Wars there were two major controversies which sharply divided Ealing's residents. Both are now forgotten, but one still resonates in the early twenty-first century; the other is now wholly irrelevant. Yet they evoked strong passions as both concerned moral and religious issues as well as attracting figures of national renown to argue the case in either side.

The first concerned the decision in December 1932 by the Maternity and Child Welfare Committee of Ealing Council to assent to a birth control clinic to be established in the council's health centre in Mattock Lane, based on the Ministry of Health's recommendations of 1930. It was agreed in principle on 13 December 1932 and the committee had to then decide on the practicalities. On 30 December the decision was made. This would entail the holding of such a clinic on one Friday afternoon per month. It would be for married women only and those who regularly attended health centres unless their doctor advised them that another pregnancy would be dangerous to their health. Dr Joan Malleson would be paid £2 2s for each session she oversaw and would have the assistance of a health visitor. The council would buy necessary equipment but if the patients themselves needed such for personal use, they would have to foot the bill.

Not all of the committee was happy with this. Councillor Scott and Mrs Emily Taylor disagreed with the proposals, but as a minority could be safely discounted.

Some local organisations backed the council. The Ealing Women's Citizens league declared, 'That this meeting urges the Ealing Borough Council to take immediate steps to provide Birth Control information', but 'the arrangements proposed are to apply only to married women who are either expectant or nursing mothers and in whose cases any further pregnancy would be detrimental to health'. Some other women's groups had similar views, such as the Holy Cross Women's fellowship and the Hanwell, Ealing and Greenford Townswomen's Guild, as did local branches of the Labour and Co-operative Parties and the Brentham Institute. They stressed the importance of preserving women's health and avoiding additional burdens on the rate payers.

A packed meeting at Ealing Town Hall noted that 'it is gratifying that the council did not yield to reactionary pressure brought against it in this connection'. Dr Marie Stopes, author of the controversial book *Married Love* in 1918 and instigator of the first British birth control clinic in 1921, spoke out on its behalf.

Those opposing tended to do so on Christian grounds, that to interfere with human reproduction was to interfere with God's plans. Numerous branches of the church-based Mothers' Unions, Christian organisations and most of the clergy were opposed. Their arguments were that 'any interference with God's law is bound in the end to prove dangerous to the wellbeing of the state, and calculated to bring about is

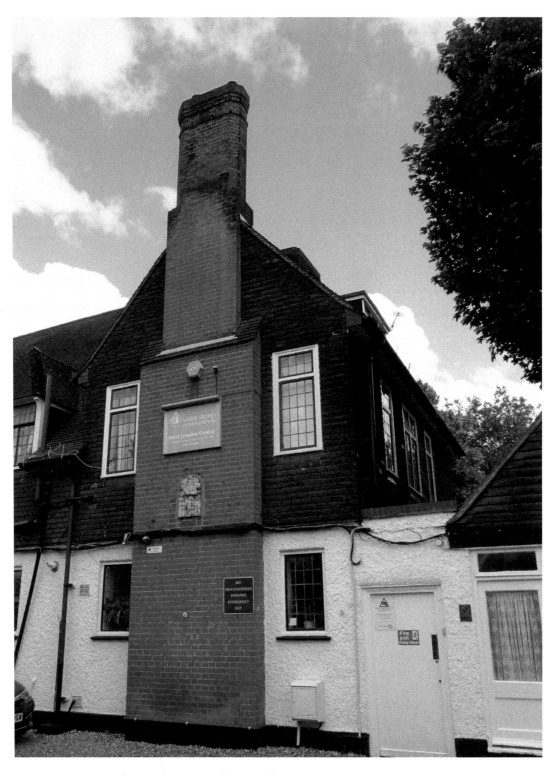

Marie Stopes Park View clinic, Mattock Lane, Ealing.

its disruption'. Secondly, they emphasised that birth control could be brought about, not by such clinics, but by 'inculcating principles of self-control and self-respect in both sexes, principles which are the hard-won victories of Christian civilisation'. The council's Medical Officer of Health should not, they believed, 'take the place of the most High God'.

This line of attack was savaged by some of those who supported the clinic's potential work. They likened the Christian defence to one which would oppose uprooting weeds from the garden. A meeting at St Joseph's Hall in Hanwell was attacked by a Mrs Cocker who claimed 'if such is the Roman Catholic attitude to a question of public policy, then God save us all from it'. She said those supporting the clinic were allegedly 'stopping ladies from having babies', turning the nursing profession into harlots and forcing their plans 'into the bedrooms of ratepayers'. She also said that the meeting's leader, the Monseigneur Barton, was unable to find where it stated in the Bible that contraception was against God's wishes.

It is hard to know where majority opinion lay and both sides claimed that they enjoyed it. At one meeting in the town hall of 900 people on 3 February 1933, only twenty-one people dissented to the motion that the council rescind its resolution to establish a clinic. Another meeting at the Queen's Hall saw a mere seven dissensions. Earlier, on 25 November 1932, a meeting supporting the clinic alleged there was 'a well-attended meeting' and only one dissension. Those opposing the clinic suggested that the council hold a referendum on the subject, but this never happened.

The protests against the clinic were of no avail. It was established, and has, over the years, expanded its remit to include abortion as well as contraception, and this has brought about controversy so great that the council has banned peaceful protest there.

The second case was similarly controversial, though very different to the first. In the 1920s and 1930s the major medium of entertainment was the cinema, especially in the 1930s when 'talkies' replaced silent films. Most people went to the cinema every week and many went more than once. It was a major leisure time occupation for all classes, sexes and ages. By the 1930s there were nearly twenty cinemas throughout what is now the London Borough of Ealing and the local press usually devoted a page to cinema adverts and reviews. It was big business and very popular.

The controversy came about because cinemas and many parks were closed on Sundays in Ealing in the 1930s (though not in neighbouring boroughs Southall and Acton). Councils had the power, from 1932, to grant licences for places of entertainment and Ealing did not grant permission for cinemas to be open on Sundays. On this day most shops were closed, as were parks, so with the exception of churchgoing, there was little to do outside the home on a Sunday (and not much to do inside it either). However, because of all this, most of the workforce (including many servants) were free on Sundays and so wanted to make the most of their limited leisure time. By 1939 all the boroughs and districts in Middlesex allowed cinemas to open on Sundays – all except Ealing.

Churchgoing and the influence of the Church was still strong in Ealing, compared to neighbouring boroughs. Sunday was the Lord's Day and indeed work was explicitly

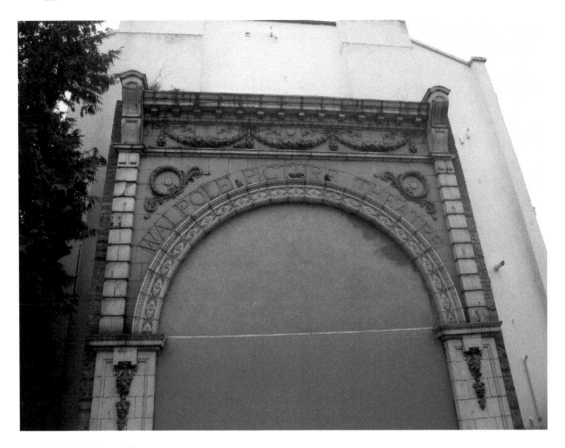

Walpole Picture Theatre.

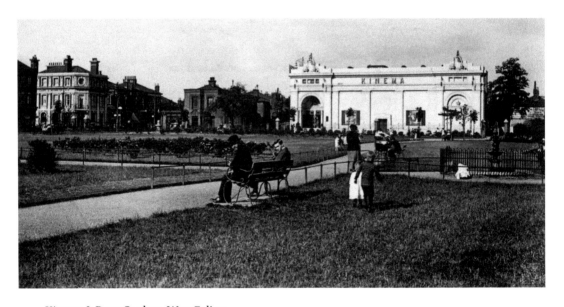

Kinema & Dean Gardens, West Ealing.

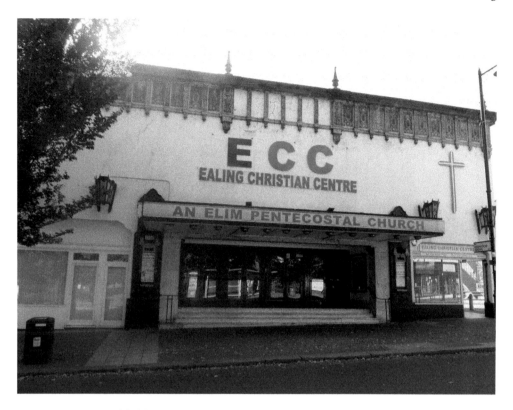

Former cinema, Northfield Avenue.

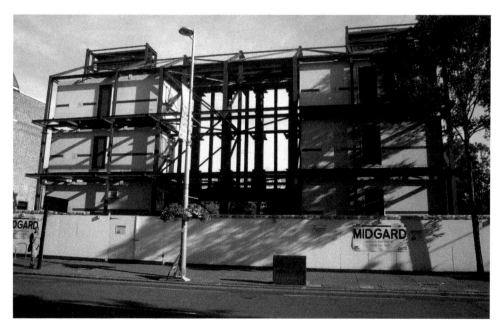

Former cinema (Forum), Ealing.

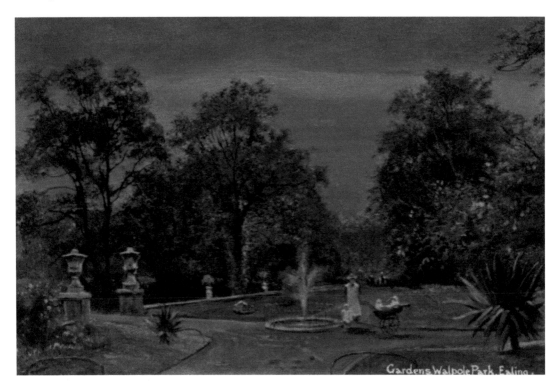

Gardens, Walpole Park, Ealing.

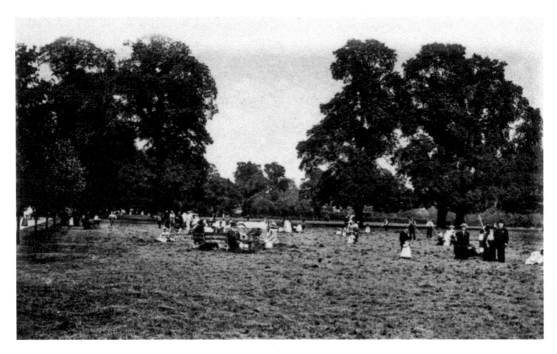

Haymaking, Walpole Park, Ealing.

banned on Sundays according to the Ten Commandments. Mr H. H. Martin was secretary of the Lord's Day Observance Society and an Ealing resident. In a meeting at the town hall he urged the audience,

> For a ness of pagan pottage
> Shall we let our Sundays go?
> Holding aloft my Bible I cry out never
> And old Ealing thunders no.

A petition of 500 people requested a poll. Ealing Council resolved to solve these problems by means of local referenda. Due to the Munich crisis, the decision over Sunday games playing was postponed from September to November 1938. The position was, that in the parks in Greenford, Perivale and at Gunnersbury games could be played on Sundays but they could not be in Ealing and Hanwell after 2 p.m. on that day. Supporters of allowing such claimed it was unchristian of Christians to oppose it. Opponents declared that this was merely the thin end of the wedge and that if games could be played in parks on Sundays, then other activities would be permissible on Sunday and so that day would no longer be any different from any other rather than as a day of worship and rest.

Voting for Sunday opening of parks (after 2 p.m., and only in reference to those parks in Ealing and Hanwell) occurred on at Ealing Town Hall and Cherington House for each day of the week beginning 26 September, but only 4,475 people turned out to vote, or around only 5.5 per cent of the total electorate. It was a very close call, with 2,313 voting against Sunday opening and 2,139 voting in favour. There was a majority of 174 voting against, therefore. Apparently 419 vote papers had not been correctly filled in and so were disallowed. It was claimed that the voting papers were not clear – not a simple yes/no, but the voter had to tick or cross the boxes next to the name of the six parks listed. Mr Fenwick was very angry with what he saw as the unfair nature of the poll, castigating 'the Kill Joy dictators of the Borough of Ealing', claiming it 'has never catered for the healthy open air pastime of its residents'.

Those against the Sunday opening of cinemas emphasised that Sunday was the Sabbath day. As a well-known Ealing resident, Florence Deane, reminded people, 'Keep it holy'. Another argued similarly that if cinemas were open on Sundays, it would 'break down the distinctive character of this hallowed day'. A young man wrote that he did 'not want the last remaining stronghold of moral strength' to be lost 'for want of a little thought'. It was also noted that the cinema industry was wealthy enough to spend a great deal on advertising.

Those arguing for Sunday opening had various arguments. Curiously enough several clergymen were in favour, arguing that people could go to church and then go to the cinema. Some argued that Ealing was 'out of step in this century'. It was surely better that young people were in cinemas than roaming the streets and causing trouble. Having worked on the other days of the week, people needed a release from the stresses of life and work and this could be found by seeing a film in a cinema on Sunday. Some people claimed that they had no wish personally to go to a cinema on a Sunday but felt that other people, especially non-churchgoers, should have that freedom to do so if they wished and those opposed to cinemagoing were not forced to go, but should show toleration to those who did.

The referendum on Sunday cinema opening occurred between 8 a.m. and 9 p.m. on 9 May 1940 at eighteen places throughout the borough, ironically on the eve of another major war-related crisis. On a 20 per cent turnout, the results were overwhelming: 13,293 for and 5, 814 against, giving those in favour a majority of 7,479.

Cinemas were given permission to open on 10 November 1940. It is worth noting that some residents were wholly unconcerned in these matters; Ealing resident and churchgoer Erica Ford in her 1940 diary doesn't refer to it at all.

3. Crime

Ealing has never been seen – historically at least – as a centre of notorious crime, as perhaps Notting Hill and Whitechapel have been, associated as they have been with well-known serial killers. However, nowhere has been free of serious crime and Ealing is no exception, and four of Britain's most infamous killers have connections with the locality.

The first is questionable, but there was a Jack the Ripper postcard delivered to Ealing Police Station on 29 October 1888 at the height of the Ripper scare, after at least four women had been killed and mutilated in Whitechapel and Spitalfields. It read as follows:

> To the High St. Ealing Police Sergent
> Beware there is two women I want here they are bastards and I mean to have them. My knife is still in good order it is a students knife and I hope you like the kidney. I am Jack the Ripper.

The writer was clearly making a link between the killer and someone with medical knowledge and also alludes to the kidney sent to George Lusk, chairman of the Whitechapel Vigilante Committee. Needless to say there were no Ripper murders in Ealing. It is highly improbable that this card was written by the killer but another hoaxer.

On the same day a letter with an Ealing postmark was sent to Poplar Police Station with a similar message:

> Dear Boss,
> I am going to commit three more murders, two women and a child – and I shall take their hearts out this time.
>
> Yours truly, Jack the Ripper.

Apparently 'the police do not attach serious importance to it'. The phrase 'Dear Boss' was taken from an early missive sent to the police, and which was the first to use the infamous nom de plume of the killer. Who the hoaxer/s was is unknown.

There was also a full report in the Acton Gazette on the death of a man who was once a prime suspect as being Jack the Ripper. This was because his body washed up from the Thames near Chiswick. Curiously his name was not mentioned in that newspaper, but from other evidence we know it was Montague John Druitt, a teacher and barrister who committed suicide in December 1888 over fears he had inherited his mother's insanity.

Secondly there was John Reginald Halliday Christie (1899–1953), serial killer of six women at No. 10 Rillington Place, Notting Hill, between 1943 and 1953. In September 1924, having recently left the RAF, he had become a petty thief as an alternative to work.

He stole from an Uxbridge cinema where he had once worked and also stole a boy's bicycle in Hillingdon – the latter he sold to a dealer in Hayes. However, resting in Southall Park, he was spotted by a sharp-eyed detective and arrested. Protesting his innocence and accusing another man who he could only vaguely identify, he was found guilty and sentenced to nine months' hard labour at Uxbridge Magistrates' Court. This gaol sentence did nothing to deter him and he committed other crimes in 1929 and 1933 before descending to murder in 1943. He was hanged in 1953 for killing his wife in the previous year. Ironically the family of his fellow tenant at Rillington Place lived in Greenford in the 1960s. Furthermore, Christie's second victim, Muriel Eady (1912–44), lived in Acton in the 1930s, at No. 48 Cresswick Road and Christie worked at the Ultra Radio Works in north Acton as a delivery and despatch driver in 1943–46 and it was there that he met Muriel.

The third link to Ealing is the case of would-be inventor and businessman John George Haigh (1909–49), better known as the Acid Bath Murderer. (He killed six people for their money and then dissolved their bodies in acid.) He had dealings with an Ealing business, Flextol Engineering Company on Ealing Green; this was over one of his innocent inventions, a silent hammer. The firm was interested but thought that it needed extra work. Naturally after his arrest for murder in 1949 the firm kept quiet! He was hanged for murder in 1949.

The corpses of two of the victims of the 1960s serial killer known as Jack the Stripper were deposited within Acton. On 14 July 1964 the corpse of thirty-year-old Scot Mary Fleming was found outside No. 48 Berrymede Road, Acton, in the early hours, by George Heard,

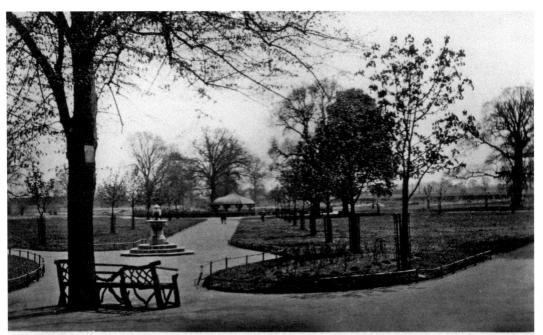

PUBLIC PARK. SOUTHALL.   No. 5

Public park, Southall.

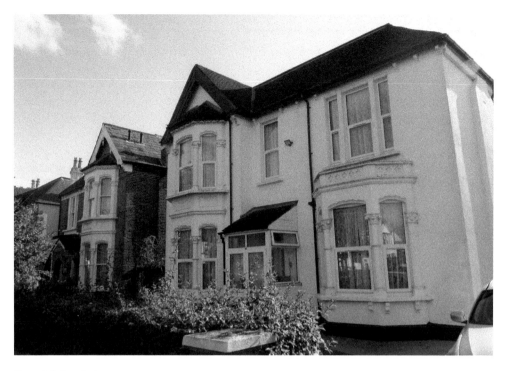

Creswick Road, Acton.

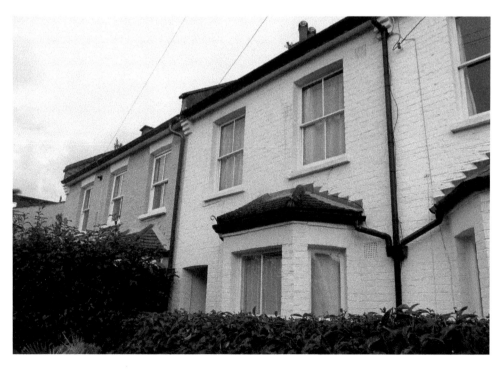

Berrymede Road, Acton.

a chauffeur on his way to work. Despite thinking it was a tailor's dummy, he had a closer look and then called the police. Undoubtedly the corpse had been dropped by the car-driving killer, having been already strangled and stripped, earlier that morning, as attested by two residents who heard the sound of a car stopping and then driving off between 2 and 3 a.m. The only clue, as with the previous victim, were traces of white paint on the body. All writers on the case have stated the body was found in Chiswick as the postcode was W4, but part of south Acton is in W4 and a glance at the borough boundaries makes it clear that Berrymede Road is in Acton.

In the following year, on the Heron industrial estate in Alliance Road, north Acton, the murderer's final victim, twenty-eight-year-old and married Irishwoman Bridget O'Hara of Hammersmith, was discovered in the same condition as Mary. Leonard Beecham, a factory employee, found the corpse at 11 a.m. on 16 February between a storage shed and the Central Line between North and West Acton stations. She had been covered by a tarpaulin and had last been seen on 11 January. She had been stored in a warm place between death and discovery and as with Mary bore evidence of white paint. Presumably the killer had stored his victims in a place where paint strippers/sprayers were used, probably a garage.

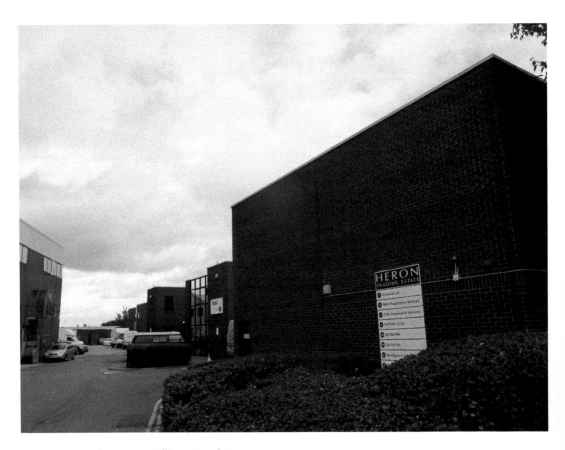

Heron Trading Estate, Alliance Road, Acton.

One suspect was Kenneth Archibald, the caretaker of a club in Holland Park, who confessed to the crimes and described how he had killed one of the women. He made several appearances at Acton Magistrates' Court (now defunct) on Winchester Road. The evidence he gave certainly was in accordance with the known facts but he eventually switched his pleas to one of 'not guilty' and whilst he was being held there was another murder in the series. He was released. The real killer had killed at least six victims between 1964 and 1965 and possibly more, dating back to 1963 or even 1959, all in west London. Although his identity has been speculated about (the suspects including a security guard, a policeman, a former Welsh child killer and an ex-boxer), it has never been confirmed.

There have also been two more recent mysteries in Ealing. One was a murder, occurring on 20 July 1988, of Diana Stafford Maw. She was a thirty-six-year-old born in Northumberland and educated at the Cheltenham Ladies' College, and was now a management consultant for the Industrial Society with premises in central London. She was found dead on the landing outside her flat in No. 24 Stanley Court, Woodfield Road, Ealing, where she had lived since 1983. There was a crossbow bolt in her head. She had been killed between 8 and 11.30 that morning, as she was on her way to work and had been shot at close range. A young neighbour found the body and was traumatised by the

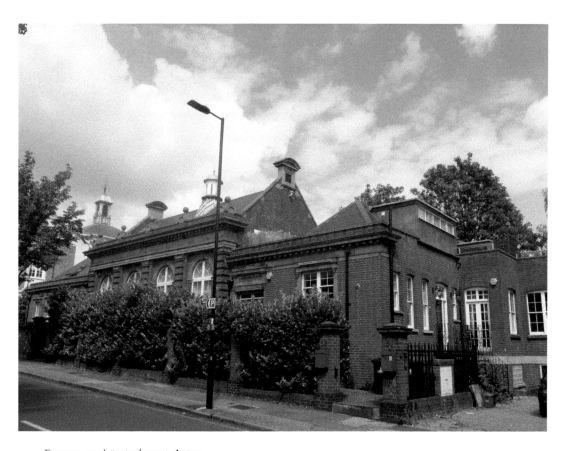

Former magistrates' court, Acton.

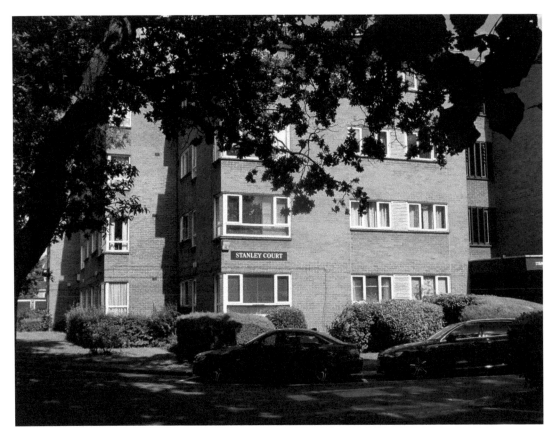

Stanley Court, Woodfield Road, Ealing.

sight. Diana had been planning to move into a house in nearby Mount Avenue, Ealing, with her boyfriend, thirty-seven-year-old businessman Michael Stevens. She had been receiving anonymous phone calls prior to her death. Recently items had been stolen from her car: a briefcase and a Filofax diary. Whether this was connected to her death or was a coincidental theft is unclear.

Diana was well liked and respected by all who knew her. She helped old people and was a keen sportswoman, being an active member of Ealing Golf Club. She had not left a will, but left around £181,000 in assets, presumably mostly her flat, on death. A memorial service was held for her at St Peter's Church in Ealing. Detective Superintendent Malcolm Hackett, who also investigated the disappearance of Suzy Lamplugh in 1986, led the investigation.

Ironically, after a spate of thefts at the flats, the residents had had a security door installed to prevent non-residents wandering into the flats. Unfortunately, this was kept open in the mornings to facilitate access for tradesmen. A third of a mile from the flat was found, in the undergrowth near a footpath by Mount Avenue and Hillcrest Road, Diana's handbag. A small red car had been seen driving from the car park of Stanley Court on the morning of the murder.

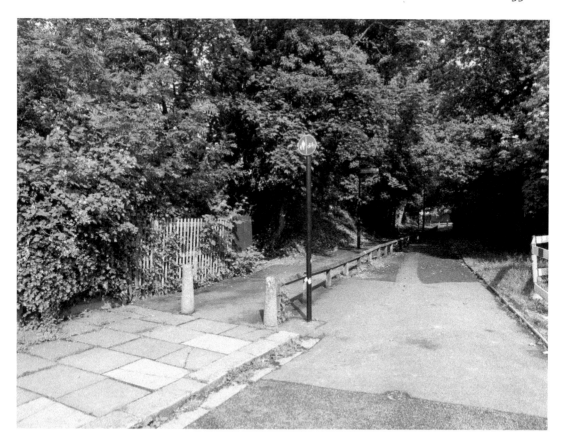

Footpath by Mount Avenue and Hillcrest Road, Ealing.

Yet it was a woman who was charged with the murder on 30 November. Jane Salveson was a thirty-five-year-old design consultant and a former girlfriend of Michael Stevens. She had a first class degree from Leicester Polytechnic and also an MA as well as a good track record in her chosen profession. She lived in Brook Green, Hammersmith. The two had become close in 1982, meeting on the Isle of Wight, where Michael, who was separating from his wife, owned a yacht. However, on 14 February 1988 Michael had met Diana and clearly preferred her to his current girlfriend, and the two split in May. Jane had trouble dealing with this traumatic experience.

She was alleged to have become so obsessed with the woman who had replaced her that she had taken to following them around and visiting their homes whilst they were out. However, she denied threatening anyone or directly confronting the new couple. A witness picked her out of an identity parade. She was remanded in custody at Holloway Prison until 22 December before being released on bail. Yet the charge was dropped the following year as the hearing at Ealing Magistrates' Court on 20 April 1989 noted that she was in the company of seven other people at the time of the murder. Charges were later brought against her in the following year for having stolen items from Michael, but these were dropped. Apparently, a man with a crossbow had been seen by an ice-cream salesman in the vicinity of Woodfield Road a few days previously and on the day of the murder. Who killed Diana and why remains a mystery? It was an unusual method of murder and it is uncertain what the motive was – an attempted robbery, perhaps, rather than anything personal against Diana?

Another mysterious event in Ealing was the disappearance of Commander Peregrine Hennicker-Heaton, born in 1903. Having served in the RAF during and after the Second World War, he retired in 1958 with the rank of Wing Commander. Hennicker-Heaton had a special interest in the Middle East and was on the council of the Anglo-Arab Association. He was married to Margaret, his second wife, with two children and lived at No. 14 Woodville Road, a fourteen-roomed house in Ealing. And then on 5 October 1971 he disappeared. His family reported him missing to the police, after having conducted a search of the property. There appeared to be no obvious explanation and conspiracy theories began to be aired. Had his connection with the Middle East been to blame? Was he involved in espionage? Was he kidnapped or dead? Yet there was no evidence to support either contention or to suggest he had left home of his own free will. It was a complete mystery.

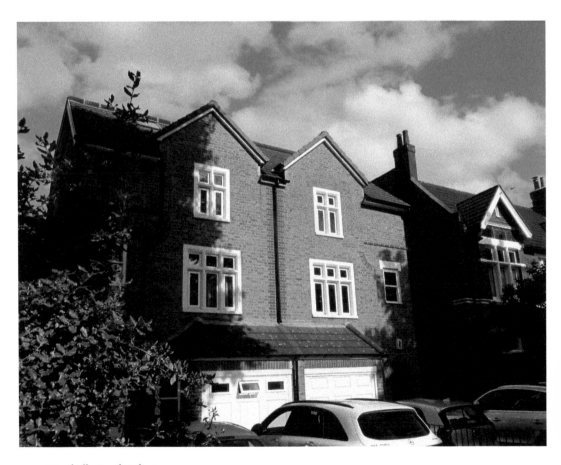

Woodville Road, Ealing.

Then on 23 June 1974, several years later, it was solved, but the solution left other questions hanging in the air. His son, Ivo, was looking for a box to store cassettes. He looked into an unused and often locked room in the house. In the room he saw on the bed what seemed to be a dusty suit but was in fact a fully clothed human skeleton! Once this was reported and the matter investigated it was clear that this was the remains of the missing baronet, as two pellets were found in the bones. However, it could not be ascertained how and why he died. It was probable that this was a case of suicide, for he had attempted this previously, once by shooting, and that he may have drunk poison.

The question, of course, is why the body had not been found in the previous three years. The room itself had been used by his daughter, Priscilla, as a bedroom until she had left for Newcastle University in 1968. Afterwards it had usually been kept locked so the dogs would not wander in there. It did not seem to have been moved and the smell of a decaying body would have been evident to the house's residents. The house had never been searched by the police and although it was made up of fourteen rooms, was hardly a mansion. It is true that nobody used the room in question anymore, but even so...

DID YOU KNOW?

Commander Peregrine Hennicker-Heaton's widow later became Mayor of Ealing, so clearly no scandal was attached to her personally.

4. Espionage

The Cold War (*c.* 1945–1990), which to those living through it then seemed a permanent state of affairs, is now but faintly remembered at local level. Hostilities between West and East predated the Second World War, however. Ealing's first known link with the spying world, which has only recently been noted, revolves around a young woman who was well known in women's local sporting circles. That lady was Olga Grey (b. 1906), who was recruited to work in MI5, infiltrating Communist and Soviet organisations and even went to India posing as a Communist fellow traveller. She was also secretary to Henry Pollitt, Secretary General of the Communist Party of Great Britain.

She was also secretary of the Ealing Ladies' Hockey Club, one of the oldest in the country, being founded in 1888, and whilst involved in this (she was also in the club's second team), in 1937, she underwent major work to infiltrate a Communist spy ring within Woolwich Arsenal, which was sending military secrets from Britain to the Soviet Union. Percy Glading was the Communist leader there and he trusted Grey implicitly. Grey gained enough information on the spies that they could be arrested and successfully convicted of treason. The work was a great mental strain and she left the service before the war and emigrated to Canada.

Indirect conflict resumed with the division of Europe in 1945, and was now at a higher ebb, with the Soviet Union being more territorially aggressive and potentially far more deadly. One of the key battlegrounds was over scientific, atomic and Space knowledge. All this may seem far removed from Ealing, which does not possess, and never did, research laboratories, code-breaking institutes or a university establishment involved in defence-related work. Acton was once home to Sean Connery when playing super spy James Bond in the 1960s, but this was fiction and far removed from the grubby reality.

Many years ago, one of the authors of this book recalled hearing in a library staffroom an elder member of staff referring to Acton Library's being often visited by members of Eastern bloc embassy officials in the 1960s and 1970s. Later the former Acton reference librarian from the 1980s recalled seeing a file marked 'The 007 file' in the cluttered office which he had inherited and proceeded to clear out. What could all this fuss have been about?

Acton in the 1950s and 1960s was a major industrial centre, perhaps the biggest in the UK south of Birmingham. It had a technical college which focussed on engineering sciences and allied trades. It was also decided that the public library's reference collection should be relevant to those studying, working and living locally. Research reports and other relevant pamphlets for scientific and atomic research would be collected, stored and made available at Acton Library.

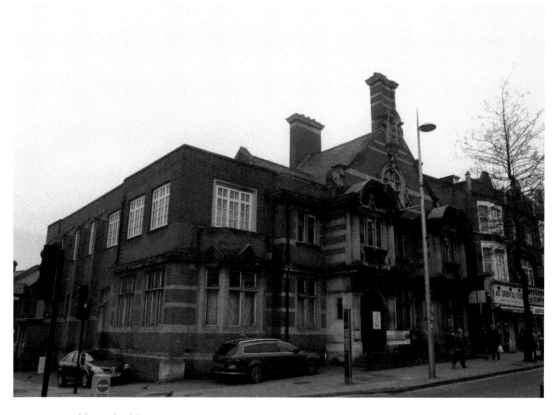

Former library building, Acton.

The potential for espionage clearly existed therefore and was not merely the product of the overheated imagination of veteran librarians. However, until 2018 little concrete could be said about this episode in local Cold War history. The file resurfaced and it shed a light on what was happening. It contains letters dating from 1968–78 to and from officials from the Ministry of Defence to Acton Reference Library. The main subject matter is that Soviet embassy officials were regularly visiting the library and asking for copies of a number of papers concerning atomic research.

A library memorandum noted on 19 December 1968,

> For at least seven years we have been receiving visits from members of the Russian Embassy staff in London. They have made use of the Library, showing particular interest in the Atomic Energy Collection.

Yet it was also noted, 'this collection does not contain any restricted material ... it is open to anyone'.

There was also a fear that library assistants and other staff might be suborned by accepting invitations to what might appear innocuous social events and they were warned about this: 'This was very necessary, as such invitations were given from time to time, notably by one A.N. Sedov, Third Secretary at the Russian Embassy and visits the Library occasionally.' In 1968 a Colonel Merkulov, an assistant military attaché, began to call on the library, with long lists of technical reports on aeronautical and aerospace matters that he wished to consult.

However, it was deemed necessary to take notice 'In view of the recent Government restrictions on Soviet diplomats in London'. A friend of the librarian, who was a former soldier, advised him to pass on information to a contact at the Ministry of Defence. The latter thanked the library for his correspondence. Names and addresses of those requesting such were also included.

And so, for the next decade, lists of publications which were requested and given to Soviet Embassy officials, with details of the latter, were sent on a regular basis to the Ministry. It is not certain how valuable this was, but there are many short letters from the Ministry, thanking them for it and noting 'It is very good of you to send us this information' and that 'it continues to be of great interest to us'. The names and addresses of the requesting officials changed over time, naturally. American journals and reports, and those on nuclear power were also requested. Such reports included, 'Experimental determination of the inertia components of an aircraft or a missile' and 'Electronic modules for aeronautics'. There were gaps when nothing was reported, such as throughout all of 1971.

A former member of Acton library staff recalled that on his first day at work in 1974 he had to sign the Official Secrets Act and was told he had to record users of this information. He was given forms detailing what was seen, time of visit, time of departure and a brief description of the man's demeanour. His first Russian visitor was Greshnikov, 'a true gentleman ... very charming' aged in his fifties; the second was Lyachenko, 'a very different Russian' in his thirties. In the following year this agent was deported after an undercover operation centred on a pub in Earls Court.

Soviet visits seem to have ceased at the end of 1977 and on 11 September 1978 the Ministry reported, 'We do not know why members of the Embassy have stopped visiting the Acton Library. We have not heard, for example, that the Embassy has turned their attention to similar libraries elsewhere.' Noting that there had been a break in 1971, they were not confident that Acton Library would not be visited again and so requested an update if and when it happened. The last letter is from the librarian, who reported, 'We shall be watching for this, and also for signs that other related Embassies are making use of the library.' As far as is known, that was the end of such visits.

Unrelated to this, as far as is known, was an Acton politician who was allegedly involved in espionage. This was Bernard Floud (1915–67), Labour MP for Acton from 1964–67. He had been involved with the Communist Party whilst at Oxford University and apparently retained Communist links until 1952. During the Second World War he introduced a War Office employee with coding secrets to the GRU attaché of the Soviet Embassy by the name Otto. After becoming an MP, he was regarded as a potential future minister and because of this he was questioned by MI5 in 1966 and 1967 by Peter Wright, as part of the security process to vet potential ministers. He described the encounter in his memoirs *Spycatcher*.

Wright thought that Floud's attitude during questioning was 'extraordinary' and that 'he treated the matter as of little importance'. Wright claimed that Jennifer Hart had been recruited by Floud to pass information to the Soviet Union. Was this true, asked Wright? Allegedly Floud replied, 'How can I deny it if I can't remember anything about it?' Wright could not give him the security clearance necessary as Floud would neither deny nor affirm the allegations. Wright believed that Floud and his now deceased brother were part of an Oxford network of spies formed in the 1930s. His relatives and friends denied that he had involvement in espionage and the MI5 investigation had not proved otherwise.

His wife Alisa died in January 1967 and this was a great personal loss for Floud. Several of those close to him recalled that he had discussed suicide and he had been unwell and off work at times throughout this year. Even so, it was a surprise for his son to find, on 10 October 1967, the dead body of his father in his bedroom in his house in Regent's Park. Uncharacteristically, he had been drinking heavily and had taken barbiturates, before turning on the gas tap and dying of carbon monoxide poisoning. Tributes from political allies and opponents came in, none having any idea that he had been investigated as a potential spy, though his level of involvement in espionage is debated.

5. Film and TV

It is no secret that Ealing possesses a film studios, and this is one of its great claims to fame, being the oldest working one in the world and that the Ealing Comedies of the 1940s/1950s were made there. Yet there are facets of Ealing's film and TV history which are less well known and these need exploring. One of the biggest myths is that the studios began life in 1902, as attested not only by numerous books but also by the studios themselves. This is untrue. Its real year of foundation, by Will Barker, was in 1907.

There are two pieces of evidence which lead to this conclusion. The first comes from the Kelly's directories of Ealing, listing businesses and householders year by year. The first time that Barker's studios are listed on the Green is in 1907 and since the evidence for these books was collected in the previous year, the conclusion is hard to resist. Yet for sceptics, there is additional evidence. In the local newspaper, *The Middlesex County Times*, there was a report in 1910 about the newly opened studios: 'It seems almost incredible that for nearly three years past, the workshop of this, the largest national business in photography should have been lying almost hidden in our midst.'

The Barker studios made many silent films, but now almost all are forgotten because they no longer survive. Set in 2.5 acres of ground, they are composed of the West Lodge and the studios built on the land. These were 'a lofty building constructed of glass so as to admit as much daylight as possible from all sides', although there was also electric lighting for evening work. There was a single stage but both sides could be used at the same time – filming on one and scenery and prop moving on the other, so as to allow filming there as soon as the first filming was done on the other. Stacks of props were located in the room, too.

A film about Henry VIII was destroyed after an agreed number of showings. Two of their epics were produced just before the First World War. One was *Sixty Years a Queen*, the first film about Queen Victoria, then Britain's longest-reigning monarch. This cost over £5,000 to make – an immense sum. Contemporary pundits were glowing: 'To Ealing belongs the distinction of having given to the cinematographic world perhaps the greatest picture that has ever been screened.' The film depicted key events in Victoria's life and reign. Although scenes from the film depicted events taking place at Westminster Abbey, Balmoral, Khartoum, the Crimea and India, the majority of these were actually shot in the studios themselves or in their grounds, though Ealing Common was also used. Two thirds of the extras were Ealing residents and many local craftsmen were employed by the studios.

Another epic which has been recently restored and was shown at Ealing Town Hall a few years ago under the aegis of the Classic Cinema Club was *Jane Shore*. This was made at Ealing Studios in 1915 and is based on a novel set during the fifteenth-century Wars of the Roses. It is historical nonsense, but is also film-making on a grand scale.

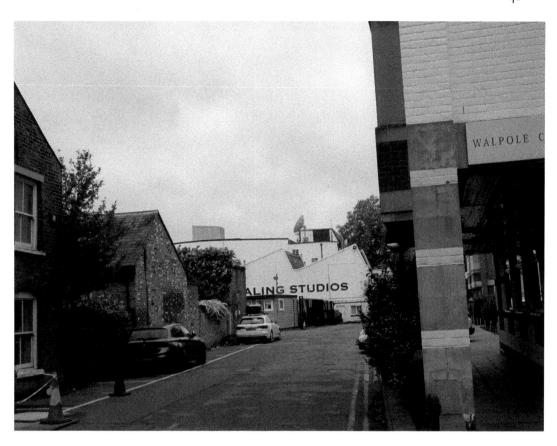

Main entrance to the Ealing Film Studios.

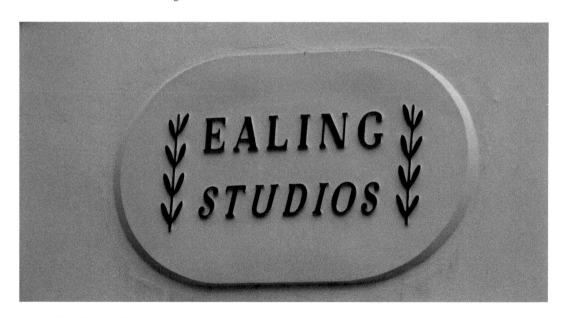

Ealing Film Studios emblem.

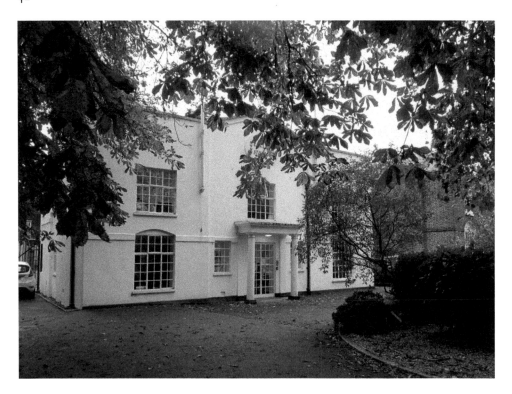

White Lodge, Ealing Green.

A total of 6,000 extras were used for battle and crowd scenes, with 342 horses, 4,500 replica weapons, and 7.5 tons of armour. It was an All-British production and deemed 'the colossal achievement of the world film trade'.

Many of the films made were rather less ambitious. Some were made by famous theatrical stars and their companies coming to Ealing and being filmed in scenes taken from plays that they had already acted in. Henry Irving once came with forty actors for the story Princess Clementine. He also performed scenes from Henry VIII, too. Sir Herbert Beerbohm Tree played the role of Cardinal Wolsey in Barker's 1911 film *Henry VIII* – he earned £1,000 a day which was an unheard-of sum to be paid at that time. Barker himself wrote scripts, such as *Luggage in Advance* in 1913, a comedy, and his brother Alfred was also a playwright. Action films were also made here. Many people sent in scenarios for films to Barker, most being rejected.

Barker ceased production in Ealing in 1925. Little known is the fact that Ealing Film Studios had offices located in Nile Lodge, Queen's Walk, Ealing, although no actual filming took place here. The Red Lion pub, opposite to the film studio, has many photos of actors displayed on the wall relating to the studios. Also the Sir Michael Balcon public house along the Uxbridge Road is another reminder of Ealing's connection to the film industry.

We should recall that there was a film studios at Southall, too, from 1928 to 1958. Relatively little is known about the studios and it never acquired the same level of fame that the Ealing Studios did. It was relatively short-lived, but it did produce a number of adverts,

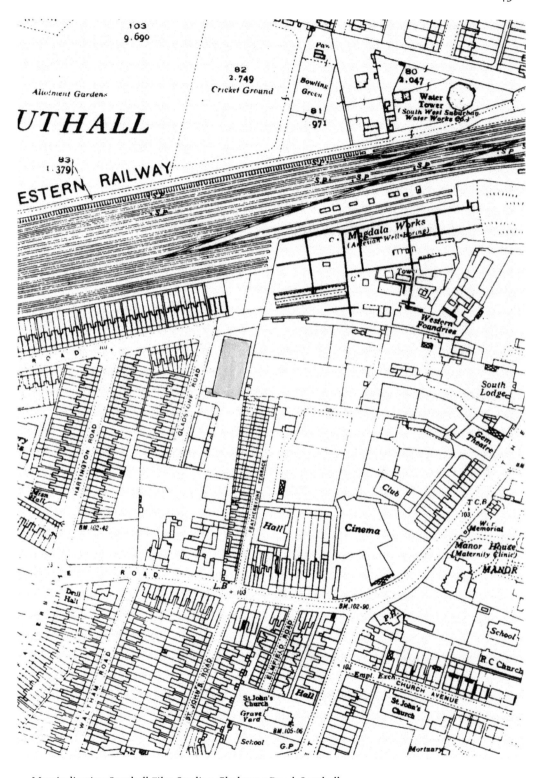

Map indicating Southall Film Studios, Gladstone Road, Southall.

films and TV shows. The Victoria Films Company opened the studios there in March 1928. The building was 'an extensive iron corrugated building' which had been built as a motor garage, but was thought to be ideal for a film studio. It did need some additional work, with carpenters and mechanics fixing up dressing rooms and other interior necessities.

Mr G. B. Samuelson, who had twenty years of experience in the film business, was the first general manager and Roy Travers was the Assistant Producer. The first film to be produced there was a melodrama starring Georgie Wood and Alma Taylor titled *Two Little Drummer Boys*. It would take four weeks to complete and used some local locations. Their next film was *For Valour*, about the history of the Victoria Cross. They were confident that there was a demand for British films and that they would do well.

In the 1930s they produced *Murder at the Cabaret* and *The Shadow Man*, as well as several Will Hay films, using locations in Southall in these films. Stuart Stross Productions made a two-reel musical film there in 1936. In the 1950s they brought out adverts and TV films for the USA and then mainly TV films for the Independent Television Authority.

It was located on the east side of Gladstone Road and was owned by a number of different organisations. From 1930–32 it was owned by the Kingsway General Films Ltd. The Britone Sound Studios was there for the next two years. By 1936 it was owned by the Metropolitan Films. It was on the night of 29 October 1936 when disaster struck and a huge fire broke out destroying £5,000 worth of equipment, though the firm claimed that they were able to save a little.

From 1945 the owners were Alliance Films Ltd, who also owned Twickenham Studios and Riverside Studios. One film made at this time was *Dancing with Crime*, starring Richard Attenborough and Shelia Sim. From 1946–54 John Grierson, a noted maker of documentary films, was Executive Producer. In 1956 the studios had three stages and forty-seven personnel. It closed in 1958. Further information can be found on a website devoted to the studios: http://www.southallfilmstudios.com/index.htm

It should come as no surprise that the borough has been the setting for many film and TV series. One of the most commonly used sites for dramas in the 1970s and 1980s was Southall Gas Works, which became redundant in 1973. It has been used in *The Sweeney*, *Return of the Saint*, *The New Avengers*, *Blake's Seven*, *Z Cars* and other dramas which needed such a setting. Stephen Pushton, locations manager for Euston Films who produced *The Sweeney*, explained why this was: 'The gas works are off the main road, away from the public and we can cosh someone over the head without too much worry. There is little interference and good parking facilities for the fleet of vehicles we have to bring, I find there are lots of nooks and crannies that make good locations and the disused buildings are useful for mocking up as small independent engineering blocks.'

Pitzhanger Manor has featured in films and dramas – not surprising since it is almost adjacent to the Ealing Studios. Its rear can be seen in the 1945 Ealing Studios film *The Dead of Night*. It has also been used in a TV adaptation of *Nicholas Nickleby*.

West Ealing and Hanwell feature heavily in the second of the Carry on films, *Carry on Constable*, which was shot in the autumn of 1959. The exterior of the police station where the hapless constables are based is actually Hanwell Library, built in 1905 and subsequently extended (interior shots are studio-based). The action takes place to the backdrop of former landmarks such as Rowses' department store on the West

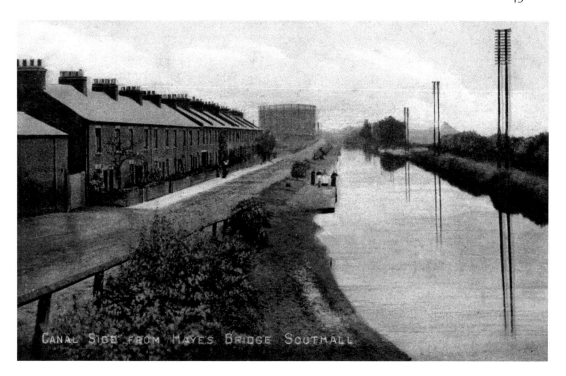

Canal side from Hayes Bridge (showing Southall Gas Works in the distance).

Ealing Broadway. St Anne's school in Hanwell, then a girls' secondary modern school, was used for the next Carry on film, *Carry on Teacher*. St Mary's Church in Ealing can be seen in the opening of a *Professionals* episode, Ealing Town Hall and the Goldsmiths' Almshouses appear in different episodes of *Minder*, whilst Ealing High Street can be glimpsed in the Autons *Dr Who* story. The Water Tower in Southall, St Bernard's Hospital and Southall Broadway all feature in episodes of the *Professionals*.

DID YOU KNOW?

A number of actors have lived in Ealing. They include David Suchet, forever associated with the role of Hercule Poirot, who lived in Cresswick Road in Acton in the 1980s and before that, in West Ealing and briefly in Southall. Fiona Fullerton lived in Norwood Green in the 1980s and Sean Connery in Acton in the 1960s, to name a few.

6. First World War

The centenary of the Great War has been and gone. Unlike the Second World War there has been no local history of this more distant conflict published. This chapter is not an attempt to rectify this, but to highlight a few of the lesser-known local elements of that conflict.

Tanks

One of the novelties of the First World War was the invention of the tank, which was to revolutionise warfare in the 1930s and 1940s. Throughout Britain, inventors were at work to produce a prototype tank in order to give Britain a military advantage in the stalemate that trench warfare had developed into by the end of 1914. It was in West Ealing that an inventor got to work.

He was Albert C. Nesfield, who had a factory on Talbot Road, employing hundreds and whose annual wage bill was £15,000. What was created was a mechanised iron box with slits for guns (rifles and machine guns) and for observation. However, the design was not adopted by the War Office.

A tank was brought outside Ealing Town Hall on 13 March 1918 in order to help raise funds for the war effort. It was known as Nelson and it 'crawled' from Acton in the morning, crawling to Chiswick the following morning. Apparently, 'it was the centre of such scenes as Ealing has never before witnessed', such were the crowds around it and at the town hall as people queued to buy war bonds from the staff inside the building. Around 6,000–7,000 people were in the vicinity of the town hall and 50,000–60,000 had lined the route. A total of almost a quarter of a million pounds was subscribed, mostly from small investors and this sum dwarfed that raised in Acton and Chiswick. The youngest investor was two days old and the whole operation was well organised by the officials and the public were orderly. The newspaper noted that the event was 'unique in the annals of the borough' and surpassed scenes seen at the Diamond Jubilee of 1897.

After the war was over, the War Office offered relics of the war such as artillery pieces and tanks to councils as war souvenirs for public display. Ealing accepted a tank in 1920 from the National Savings Association in return for the financial contribution that Ealing had made towards the war effort in their unprecedented purchase of war bonds, and it was decided to put it in Dean Gardens, on a specially built base. However, it became a subject of controversy as the years passed and with the rising pacifist sentiment, there were calls that the council have it removed. Some favoured its retention, such as the Ealing branch of the Royal British Legion.

In 1922 there was a letter stating that 'The tank, itself hideous, symbolises something still more hideous – war. To me, it is a monument to man's inhumanity to man.' The anonymous critic thought that it was an 'eye and mind sore', immoral, pagan and detrimental to the children who saw it. He wanted it scrapped. Yet others took a different view. A local war veteran claimed 'One cannot but admit that the tank is ugly and gloomy, but I feel sure that many will agree that the statement that it is also useless is not correct.' He saw it was 'a constant visible indication that Ealing as a borough did its "little bit" in the great war and that the manhood of the borough were eager and ready to do its duty'. It was an object of pride, stirred the conscience of slackers and would inspire youngsters to do their duty in the future. There were many other letters and the last one being by the first writer who wanted a monument to the nurses of the war to be placed there instead, being answered by a critic 'leave the tank alone'.

The subject was dropped until a council meeting in October 1932. Councillor Fuller wanted it removed and sold as scrap metal. Councillor Garner pointed out that it was a source of local pride, Nesfield having designed a tank not far from where the tank stood. He read out letters from local chambers of commerce, from Nesfield and an ex-servicemen's group in favour of its retention. Some councillors who had served in the war claimed that it brought back grim memories of Passchendaele and that the tank was 'the most diabolical weapon ever invented'. It was not a source of pride locally but a shameful thing. The council voted for its removal and a Norman Roberts of No. 23 Winscombe Crescent wrote 'The borough will be well rid of it.' Ernst Hodges of Lynton Gardens disagreed: 'It is difficult to understand the mentality of those who acted in this manner, but let us be charitable and conclude that they meant well.'

Air Raids and Fear of Raids

It is well known generally that the Second World War led to the Blitz of 1940–41 on London and the resultant loss of life and property in London on a scale not known since the seventeenth century. What is less appreciated is that German zeppelins and bombers raided London on frequent occasions between 1915 and 1918, killing hundreds and spreading fear, by this unprecedented method of warfare against the civilian population far away from the front lines.

Although much of the bomb damage fell on the East End and central London, as it was to do so in 1940–41, other residents on the outer suburbs were also worried about the potential danger to which they were exposed. In June 1915, a concerned resident of Acton wrote, 'When are the people of Acton going to be instructed how to act in case of an air raid?' and said that the council, 'who are the civic parents of the citizens' needed to let them know so as to avoid panic.

There were further concerns in the summer of 1917. One man found two large barrels on his allotment and feared that they had been dropped by aircraft, keen to lighten their load, but they turned out to be quite innocuous. On 7 July, during an air raid, female employees from Messrs Lyons and Wrench took shelter in Acton Wells School. Three days later the school formally applied for such permission that 120 might be allowed to shelter in the hall on the ground floor. However, the school authorities were opposed to this because of the disruptive effect it would have on the pupils' schooling. Shelterers were only allowed in school premises if it was outside school hours and that the sheds in the playground which should be proof against shrapnel, could be used.

Riot

During the war there was, naturally, a great deal of anger directed against Germany and Germans, of which there were a few in the locality, leading to Germans being interred for fear that they might aid the German war effort and German names being changed; thus locally Heidelburg College in Ealing became Harvington College, the King of Prussia pub on Southall Green became The Victory but Altenburg Road remained Altenburg Road.

Yet the response became violent in Acton. This was triggered by the unprecedented sinking by a German submarine of the civilian ship the *Lusitania*. The loss of civilian life was deemed outrageous – a war crime and thus justice was deemed essential. German shops were attacked throughout the country. This may have been restricted to Acton rather than Ealing and elsewhere, because two Acton residents had been on board the doomed ship and one of them had drowned. This was reported in the local newspaper.

On Tuesday 11 May, between 1,500 and 2,000 people – men, women and boys – armed themselves with missiles and congregated outside a German shop on Bollo Bridge Road. They then broke the windows of the German baker's shop. On the following evening, at 7 p.m., 2,000 people gathered and attacked five different shops, scattered between Churchfield Road, The Vale, Church Road and Park Road North. Despite police patrols, windows were broken as before, but there were no thefts or assaults. The crowd cheered as they wreaked violence and sang patriotic songs. One refrain was 'Pay them back for the Lusitania', this making their motive or perhaps their justification explicit. They even marched to Ealing to continue their endeavours, but a strong police presence in Ealing Broadway prevented them from doing so.

The final day of the rioting was on 13 May. Again the crowd assembled, this time of Acton High Street. Yet now the police were concentrated and so no violence occurred. The crowd began to drift away and so ended the Acton anti-German riots.

Seven people had been arrested and were brought before Acton Magistrates' Court. The accused claimed that they had been carried away by anti-German feelings. One girl claimed she had brothers who were fighting at the Front and that she and her fellows were merely doing the government's work for them. Whilst the magistrates could understand the sentiments behind the violence they stated that this was not the way they should express them. Men could enlist to fight. The defendants were given minor fines, but warned that any future similar behaviour would be dealt with more harshly.

Ernest Woollff, a dentist practising on the Vale, was angry about the rumour that he was German and said he would pay £50 to whoever could tell him who the rumour-monger was so that he could have him prosecuted. One shopkeeper, though of German descent, had it known that he was born in England.

This has been Acton's only riot.

DID YOU KNOW?

Other businesses were eager to show that that they had no German affiliation. Beauchamp and Sons stated 'only British labour employed' and Parker and Son on the High Street proclaimed 'A British Firm carried on by British Labour'.

Fatalities

There is only one female name on the Ealing war memorial outside Pitzhanger Manor – 'Miss A. Harman'. Alice Maud Harman was born in 1891 and lived with her family at No. 1 Glenfield Road, West Ealing. She had been employed as a servant but on 4 November 1916 joined the workforce of Llewellyn Dent and Co. at Warple Way, Acton. Whilst at work

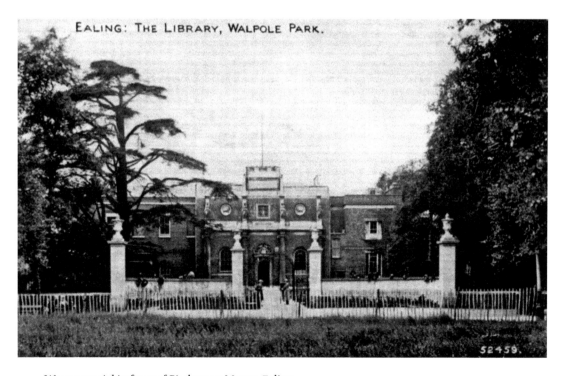

War memorial in front of Pitzhanger Manor, Ealing.

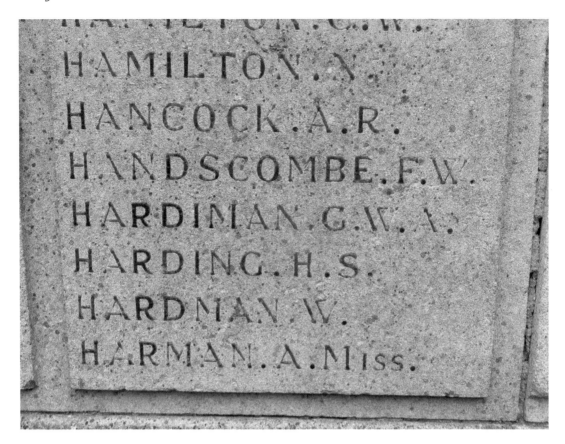

Miss A. Harman.

in this munitions factory, on 23 December, she was taking a break in the canteen and whilst making tea, her oily overalls caught fire. Thinking that a bucket of water would put these out, a fellow employee tossed the liquid over her, not realising that it was, in fact, paraffin, and Alice's fate was sealed. The inquest found that this was an accidental death and it was Ealing's only female fatality in the First World War. A similar fate overtook sixteen-year-old Acton girl Dorothy Maud Crowther in 1918 when she died in a munitions factory accident.

Another of the war's unusual fatalities in the locality are the two Russian airmen who were buried in Southall Cemetery in 1917. These were Cadet George Smirnov who died on 26 June 1917 and his compatriot Novikov who was killed on 16 September in the same year. Both were learning to fly with the British Royal Flying Corps at an unspecified aerodrome nearby, but which was probably the newly established Northolt Aerodrome. Smirnov was in an aeroplane with Captain Waine, an instructor, when the airplane crashed and though Smirnov was taken from the machine, he later died at the Southall Australian Hospital at the former St Marylebone School. (Waine was killed in the crash.) Novikov, who had a hitherto good record of flying, had his airplane go into a nosedive and was burnt to death when the plane crashed. He was twenty-four years of age.

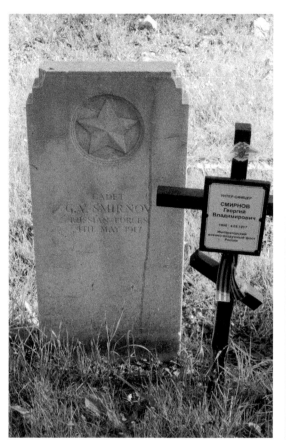 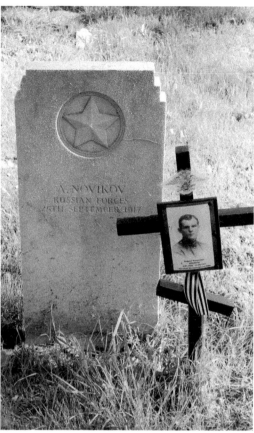

Above left: Russian airman G. V. Smirnov. (Colin Harris)

Above right: Russian airman A. Novikov. (Colin Harris)

7. Mental Health

Diseases of the mind were traditionally kept under wraps and it has only been relatively recently that the issue has increasingly come under a less unsympathetic spotlight. Indeed, a publication produced in 1904 about Ealing boasted that, apart from positive attractions such as good schools, shops and transport links, there were negative attractions and these included an absence of nuisances – no workhouses, no magistrates' courts and no asylums!

Yet they did exist locally. A local symptom of this is that, although the first public asylum in what is now Greater London was established in the parish of Norwood in 1829 and although it was titled The County Asylum, it was unofficially named the Hanwell Asylum (later St Bernard's Hospital) because it was close to the village of Hanwell. Attempts were made to rename the latter because of its association with the asylum. All they achieved was to rename Hanwell railway station to Hanwell and Elthorne station.

The pioneering work there of Doctors William Ellis and John Conolly is too well known to be repeated here, but there are other facets of its history which are less well known and are thus worth noting. It was referred to in Agatha Christie's novel *The Big*

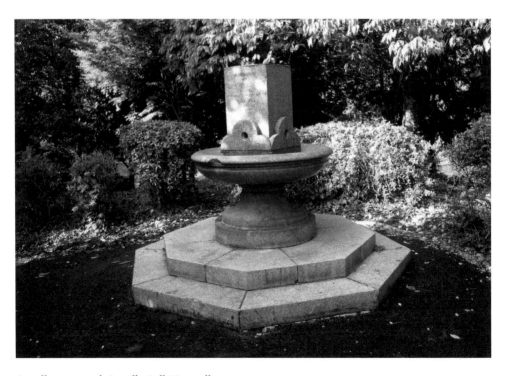

Conolly memorial, Conolly Dell, Hanwell.

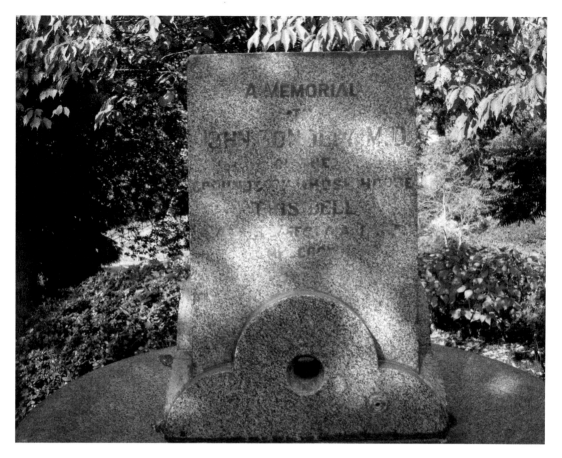

Inscription on the Conolly memorial.

Four (1927). An alleged attendant tells Hercule Poirot that a man has left the asylum and harbours numerous delusions. It turns out that the man is actually sane and has news of a major criminal conspiracy and the alleged attendant is on a mission to murder him, which he does.

Over the years there have been tens of thousands of patients there and so it should be no surprise that there have been numerous (in)famous ones. A relatively recent patient at the hospital was one who became known to one of this book's authors and was the subject of a biography by the other. That man was Donald Hume (1919–98). Arriving at the hospital in 1988 after twelve years at Broadmoor (and seventeen years in a Swiss prison), he remained for around two years to complete his rehabilitation into the outer world. Hume was a notorious double murderer and bank robber, killing Stanley Setty, a car dealer, in 1949, dismembering him and scattering his remains into the sea from a light aircraft in 1949. He literally got away with murder, but was sentenced to life in Switzerland in 1959 for shooting dead Arthur Maag, a taxi driver. However, in his time at St Bernard's, he had mellowed considerably and seemed a very polite, respectful and helpful old man, especially fond of gardening and aeroplanes.

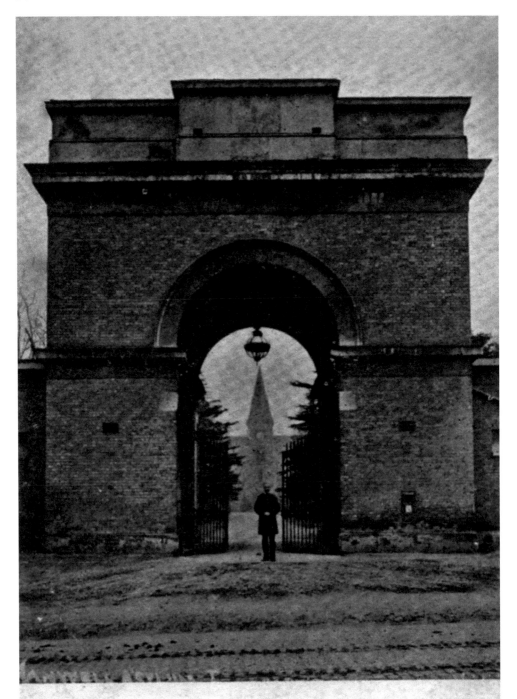

LONDON COUNTY ASYLUM (IN SOUTHALL-NORWOOD PARISH), NEAREST RAILWAY STATION, G.W.R. HANWELL.   POSTAL ADDRESS—HANWELL, W.

London County Asylum entrance.

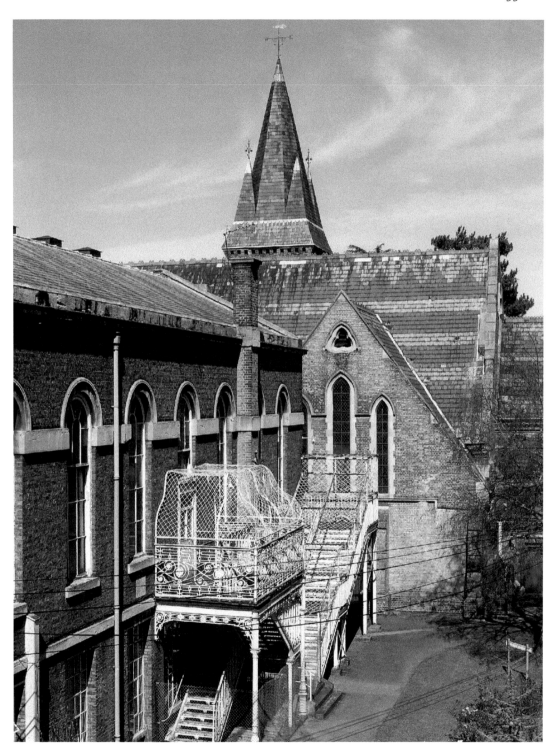

Chapel and ballroom, St Bernard's Hospital.

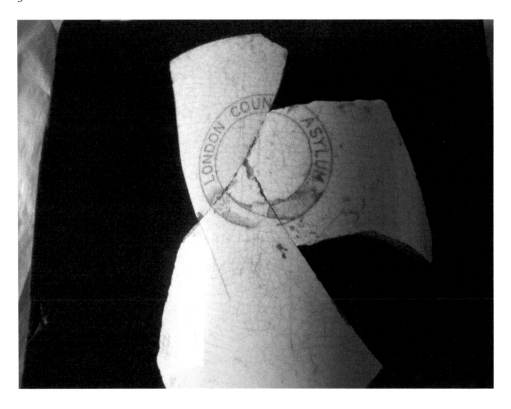

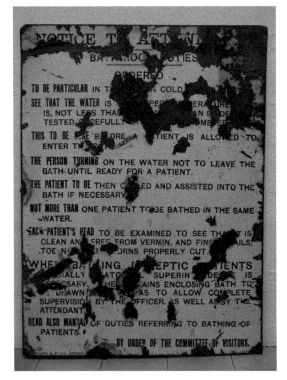

Above: London County Asylum mug. (Gunnersbury Park Museum)

Left: London County Asylum bathing instructions. (Gunnersbury Park Museum)

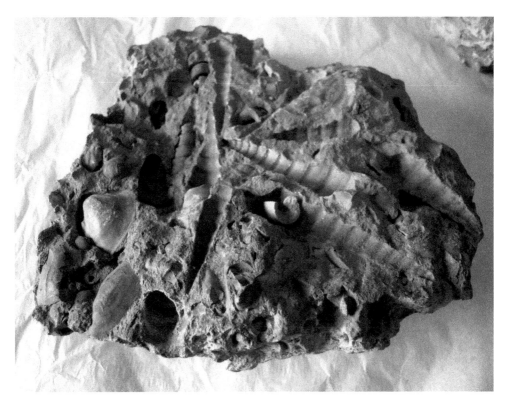

Rock and shell concretion, found at the bottom of the asylum well. (Gunnersbury Park Museum)

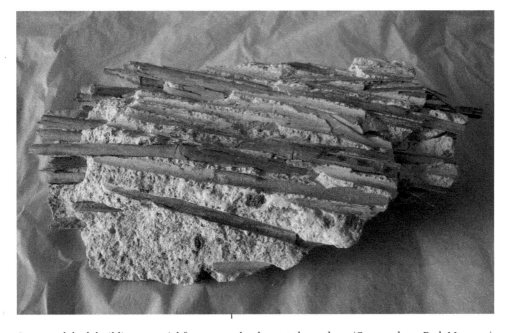

Straw and daub building material from an early phase at the asylum. (Gunnersbury Park Museum)

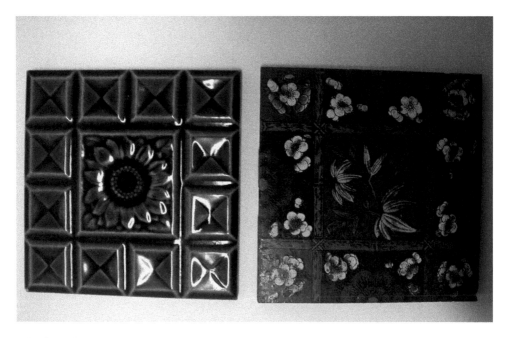

Tiles from the London County Asylum. (Gunnersbury Park Museum)

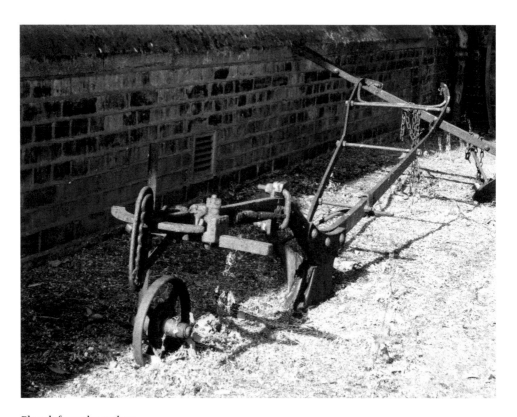

Plough from the asylum.

There have also been a number of small, shorter-lived private asylums in Southall and Hanwell in the nineteenth centuries.

Southall Park was a country house dating to the eighteenth century, just south of the Uxbridge Road and was a private asylum from at least 1838 to 1883. Its first proprietor was Sir William Ellis and its last was Dr Robert Boyd, from at least 1878. In 1881 there were ten female (two born in India, aged between thirty and sixty-seven) and eight male patients, aged between twenty-five and seventy-four (three former military men), with six servants and Boyd's family in residence. One of these men, Captain Williams, was, in 1883,

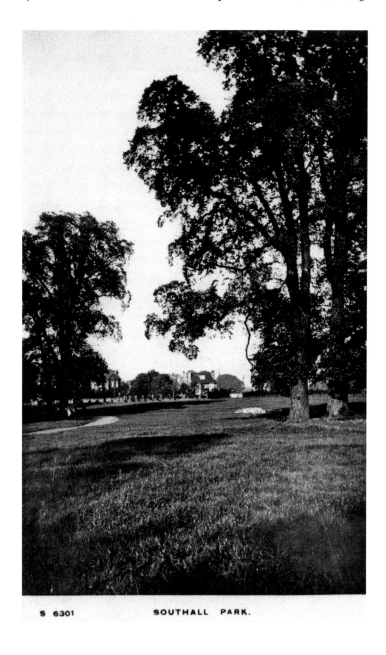

Southall Park, *c.* 1911.

S 6301   SOUTHALL PARK.

aged sixty-five and had been there for thirty years after having been mentally injured in India and was popular with his fellows. Disaster struck in August 1883 and the house burned down, with five fatalities, including Dr Boyd. The ruined house and grounds were eventually bought by Southall-Norwood Council and became Southall Park.

A lesser-known asylum in the parish, but one that did not come to such a dramatic end, was Vine Cottage, on the south side of Norwood Green. It was in existence from at least 1871–81 and was no longer there in 1886. Jessie Chalk was the proprietor; there were eleven patients in 1871 and nine in 1881, and she had six resident servants.

In Hanwell in 1839 there were two, one run by a Mrs Martha Magnell and the other by Mrs Susan Wood. Both were private asylums for female patients. The former had ceased to exist by 1845, but the latter was still there until at least 1851. It was run by Susan Woods and there were nine patients, two being widows, one was married and the rest were single. The asylum was in north Hanwell, in a house called Elm Grove, which was on Church Road (the building still exists) and near to Dr Emerton's Hanwell College. It had ceased to exist in 1861 and had then become a clergyman's residence. Dr Conolly's asylum at the Lawn held only four patients in 1851 (all female) and termed gentlewomen, aged between twenty-one and sixty-seven and three were unmarried. A small park named Conolly Dell now stands on Conolly's former garden.

Then there was Featherstone Lodge on the Green in Southall. This was initially known as Welch's Folly as it cost Alfred Welsh £20,000 to build, and took several years to do so. It had thirty-six rooms and a high wall around it. It was a private asylum for women from at

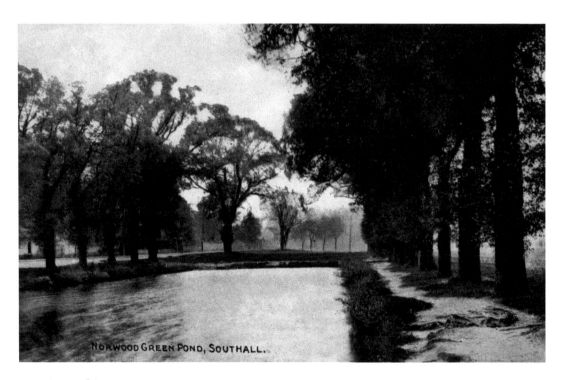

Norwood Green, c. 1907.

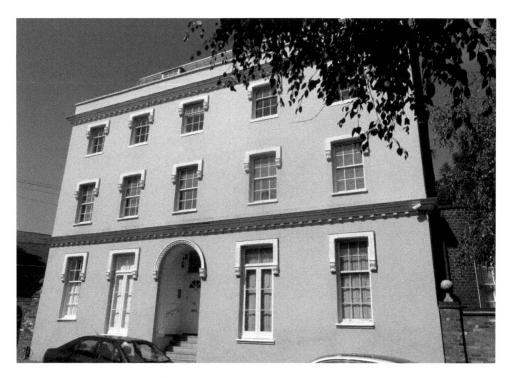

Elm Grove, Church Road, Hanwell.

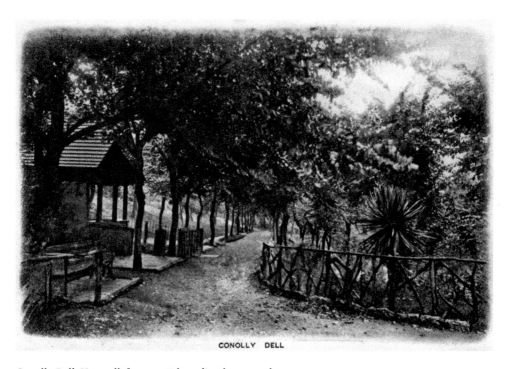

CONOLLY DELL

Conolly Dell, Hanwell, from an Edwardian letter card.

least 1894 when a Miss Dixon was the proprietor. In 1901 Hepziah Dixon was the owner. He had fifteen servants on the site and there were ten patients, all female, and aged between forty-eight and seventy-six. One had been born in Australia, one in New Zealand and two in Ireland. Seven were single, two were widows and one was married. By 1911, Dr William Henry Bailey was in charge of the ten patients, aged between twenty-five and eighty-seven. In 1924 Bailey ceased his work there and was succeeded by Alfred Newman Leathern, MRCS, LRCP, and it continued in use as an asylum until 1931. It clearly did not have a sinister reputation, for several local organisations held garden parties and fetes in the grounds in the 1920s.

It was demolished in 1935 and the Dominion Cinema opened on the site in the following year. Fifty years on it was, in turn, replaced by the Dominion Arts Centre which now houses Southall Library and Ealing local History Centre.

There was also a private asylum in Ealing, to the south-west of the Common, run by the East India Company for its employees, from 1870–92. Its superintendent was Dr Thomas Christie. Elm Grove was owned by Mrs Spencer Perceval and on 25 March 1870 was sold to the Company for £24,500, as it then stood vacant. Messrs Ashbury and Horne, contractors, were paid £11,750 13s 2d to convert it from a country house to an asylum. The asylum opened on 28 August 1870. Dr Christie was paid £800 per year and there were twenty-seven other staff; the attendants were paid £24 per year. They had 156 patients to care for, divided into first and second class, the majority being in the latter section.

The asylum closed on 24 June 1892 and was demolished shortly afterwards, once the patients had been transferred elsewhere. It is worth noting that contrary to popular fiction, the majority of women in these asylums were not married and had not been consigned there by their wicked husbands.

Finally there were two asylums in Acton. Derwentwater House on Horn Lane was built in 1807. In 1855, Sarah Binfield, with her sister Jane and seven assistants, had seven gentlewomen and one clergyman as their patients. Medical care was provided by the non-resident Dr Pearce Rogers Nesbitt. The asylum was still there in 1871, but later became the premises of a Radical Club. Also in Acton was the asylum at The Friars, from at least 1861–87. Frederick James Smee was in charge in 1871 and later, one James Bonin. Their inmates included a clergyman's daughter, a clergyman's wife (presumably not ones belonging to the same man) and a merchant's wife.

Quite why there should have been so many asylums locally is another question, but it was probably because in the nineteenth century the district was fairly rural and so land was easily available. Possibly the establishment of the county asylum in 1831 may have fixed Hanwell and Southall with asylums into the minds of those wanting to set up such. We also know little about the life of the patients there and their treatments, as no archives survive. (Census returns do not list their names, only initials, and birthplaces are rarely stated.)

8. Peopling

Twenty-first century Ealing is made up of people from many parts of the world. It was not always so, and therefore it is worth charting the early history of Ealing's peoples. Most, until the later twentieth century, were from different parts of the British Isles. Welsh, Scottish and Irish people were all predominant among the English majority. In the early twentieth century (and indeed before) there were also a number of people from India and Africa living locally.

The first known Irishmen in this district came about because of the building of the railways. It was noted that in 1836 that some of these Irish navvies were involved in fights with local people in the now defunct Stag public house in Hanwell. Many Irishmen and Welshmen were seasonal workers and were employed at the Northolt brickfields in the summer months. There were more Irish in England than any other overseas group until relatively recently. In 1921 the numbers locally were relatively small: 593 in Acton and 822 in Ealing, but by 1951 these had risen to 2,196 and 7,796, respectively. There was an Irish club in Hanwell in the 1930s.

A significant number of Scots lived in Ealing in the twentieth century so that an Ealing and District Scottish Society was formed and they were regularly noted as holding events, the most important being the celebration of the New Year, Hogmanay, which was not then a major event in the English calendar. According to the 1921 census there were 1,062 Scots in Ealing – nearly 2 per cent of the population – and in 1951 this figure had risen to 3,697. The Scottish society had 120 members in 1907 and 162 in 1958. Its chairman, Dr Fleming, in 1907 noted that the aims of the society were 'to strengthen the connection with the land to which they were born and to preserve the national characteristics of the race'. The society aimed to bring Scots living in this part of London together, especially young men working and living in the capital, to assist Scots fallen on hard times and to reinforce Scottish culture and literature. At the dinners, members invariably wore kilts, drank whisky, quoted Scottish poetry, ate haggis and a bagpiper was a must.

The depression of the late 1920s and 1930s led to a migration of people from South Wales into West London, travelling along the main railway line. Many stayed to live in Southall. As with the Indian migrants there in the 1950s they formed their own social and cultural groups in order to preserve their inherited traditions. There was a Welsh male choir founded in Southall in 1931. Frederick Priddle was one such Welshman, once employed in the mines, but when they began to decline, he went to Southall and took part in a government-sponsored training programme to learn new skills to work in industry. He became engaged to a girl who he had known in Merthyr Tydfil, who was the housekeeper to another Welshman. In 1951 the highest number of people in Southall, other than English, were the Welsh, numbering a total of 2,237 or around 4 per cent of the total population. An observer noted in 1934 that Southall's streets were 'thronged with immigrants'.

There were Welsh choral events and church services, some held in the Labour Hall on the Uxbridge Road. The major celebration, was, of course, St David's Day (1 March), which was celebrated with folk music, speeches, daffodils, leeks and the Welsh flag. The minister of a Welsh church on Ealing Green, Mr P. A. Geoffrey Davis, assisted, and in the later 1930s the mayor of Southall also graced the event with his presence, to welcome them and to state how well relations between locals and the Welsh were.

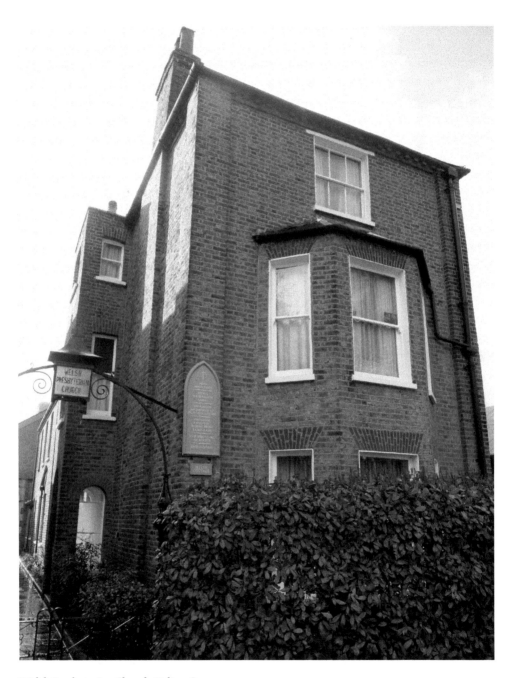

Welsh Presbyterian Church, Ealing Green.

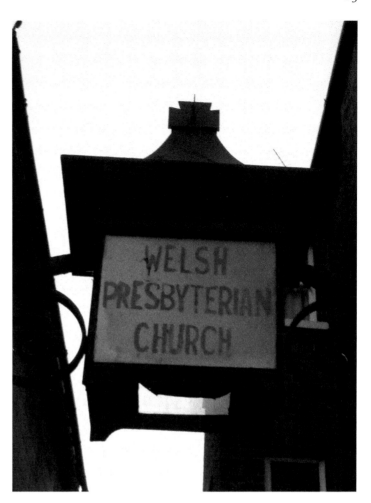

Detail of lamp, Welsh
Presbyterian Church,
Ealing Green.

There was a Welsh Sunday School opened in 1933 on South Road, Southall, behind a former Wesleyan chapel, the first in the district. This was for adults as well as children, in order to learn to speak and write in the Welsh language, in order to keep their heritage alive. It seems to have fallen into decline but was reopened in 1936.

There were even more Welsh in Ealing in the 1930s–50s. With 784 Welsh in Ealing in 1921, in 1951 this had risen to 5,398. This may have been in part due to the Welsh church on Ealing Green, but it was also due to economic factors. New industries were opening in Brentford, Perivale and Greenford along the major arterial roads. It seemed an ideal opportunity for young people to start a new life, and one such was twenty-year-old Alfred Gilbert, injured in a mining accident, and his wife, moving to a house in Conway Crescent, Perivale, where he got a job with Stowell's, an Ealing wine retailer in 1934.

Not everyone appreciated the arrival of so many Welshmen. A newspaper article of 1929 referred to the 'incursion' of Welsh into Middlesex and into Southall and Hayes in particular. It was pointed out that an English workman would want 1s 3 1/2d in wages per hour, but a Welshman would be happy for 10d for the equivalent work.

Therefore, 'the present unparalleled Welsh invasion is causing intense bitterness and heart burning amongst local working class men', although it was noted that MPs denied this. By 1937 it was thought that there were over 100,000 Scots living in London and even more Welsh, whereas in 1755 Goronoway Owen, curate at Northolt and poet, was one of the few Welshmen in, or near the Metropolis.

There were also peoples from other countries resident in the neighbourhood, too, beginning with French priests shortly after 1066. In 1921 there were 646 people in Acton who had been born in the Americas or Europe and 972 in Ealing. Of these, the largest numbers were the French, numbering 121 and 167 respectively, with 91 Germans in Acton (despite the war and anti-German rioting here in 1915) and 108 Americans in Ealing. There was also a strong contingent of former colonials in Ealing (as noted by both Agatha Christie and George Orwell), people of British descent but born in India of military, civil service, missionary and merchant families – 744 in all.

Numbers rose after 1945; in 1951 there were 5,059 people described as being born overseas in Ealing (excluding people from the Commonwealth and colonies), though in less-populous Acton there were 2,385 and in Southall 1,724.

There were very few Asian and black people in the district until the 1950s, but they were not entirely unknown even then. The first known black people locally were servants; there was a black servant girl, Sykey, at the Duchess of Hamilton's house in east Acton, who was

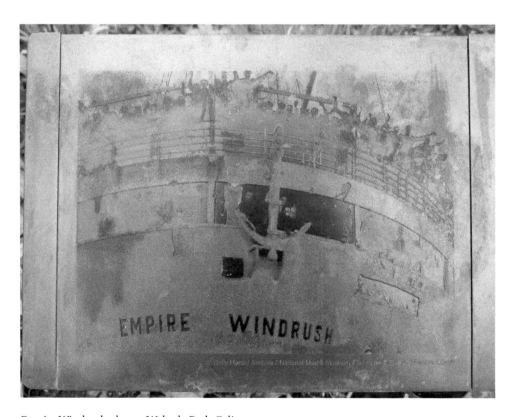

Empire Windrush plaque, Walpole Park, Ealing 1.

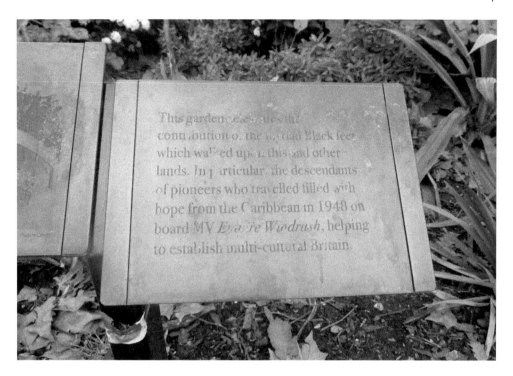

Empire Windrush plaque, Walpole Park, Ealing 2.

buried in the churchyard in 1739. Two other black people are noted in the Ealing parish registers, one being John Orincko, baptised in 1754, and the other being an adult baptism in 1811 – Thomas Dennis, aged eighteen. There were a number of black people in Ealing and Hanwell in the 1900s and 1910s. Those in Hanwell included James Richards, who was a sailor and when drunk tried to kiss a policeman outside The Viaduct pub in 1913. Another was Alexander Fraser, a bookmaker, collecting gambling monies at the Duke of York in 1905.

Better known locally was John Alexander Barbour-James, who had been employed in the African colonial service in the Post Office. He and his family settled in Acton in the 1900s and took a large part in Church affairs, firstly at All Saints' where two of his sons were in the church choir, and then at St Dunstan's, scene of his second marriage, in which all the African notables in London attended. The family lived at a house in Birkdale Grove and then at Goldsmith's Avenue from the 1920s. Once retired, Barbour-James was heavily involved in African politics in London and spoke to audiences locally and nationally. His message was that Africans were not savages, that he was not exceptional, and that with the right encouragement and help Africans could and were prospering and progressing within the framework of the British Empire, which he admired. Many of his children were musically talented and in high demand as performers. The family left the district in 1933.

A tragic case was that of Grace Stevenson, a servant who committed suicide whilst in her bridal attire at her employer's house on King's Road in April 1919 and this made front-page news in the local newspaper – 'Coloured Woman's Lament'. It transpired that her fiancé in Jamaica had jilted her, her family were asking her for more money and to

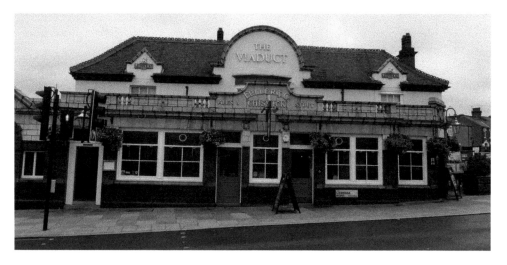

'Viaduct' public house, Hanwell.

cap it all, tradesmen's boys calling at the house had made racial jibes at her, so she decided to end it all by turning on the gas and making her room airtight.

Asian people were also few; in 1921 there were only three people in Ealing who were described as 'Asiatic Indians'. The first known Indian in Ealing was Savandar Banarjee, a student, presumably at the University of London, but resident in Florence Road in Ealing in 1911. Mrs Gupta, resident at Northcote Avenue in 1915–17, was involved in Christian missionary work to India and spoke at meetings in Ealing on the subject. She was presumably wealthy and her husband was an army officer. Another well-known Indian in this district in the 1930s was the young actor Sabu, who lived in Northolt whilst employed at Denham Studios making films such as *The Drum* and *The Thief of Baghdad*. There was also an Indian doctor in Perivale in the 1930s and an Indian cloth merchant in business there. Two affluent Indian barristers were resident in north Ealing in the 1920s, although both got in trouble with the law and so their residence here was limited. Of course, newspapers tend to report miscreants not honest, law-abiding people.

DID YOU KNOW?

There are many other people in the past in this locality who should be better known now (perhaps by blue plaques). These include Miss Susan Smee, the district's first female councillor, representing south Acton from 1910–28. She was also the first female chairman of committees, as well as the full council, mayor and was the founder of Gunnersbury Park Museum. Lady Travers Humphreys was the first female magistrate locally as well as organiser of Belgium refugee relief in the First World War. There is no local memorial to either, nor to Barbour-James, referred to above.

9. Politics

Those who know of Ealing's famous politicians will probably recall Spencer Perceval, Ealing resident and Prime Minister, 1809–12 (commemorated by a plaque on All Saints' Church) and, more recently, the less successful Neil Kinnock, of whom there is no suggestion of any commemoration. Yet between these two men have been a number of instances of politicians associated with the borough who perhaps are mostly left forgotten.

Extremist politics usually gain few supporters but plenty of attention from journalists and ill-chosen words can also attract infamy, if only temporarily. There are a few instances of such from the Far Left. In 1843 there was a reputed Communist cell in Hanwell. This was established by Norfolk-born John Goodwyn Barmby (1820–81). This was the Hanwell Morville Communtorium. Its aim was 'universal brotherhood' and sought equal education for both sexes and adult education. It sought a new world, with years dating from number one, and that equating to AD 1841. Barmby organised a Communist conference in London in 1845. He toured the country giving lectures on the topic, whilst based in a house in Half Acre. However, he was unpopular in Hanwell and in 1848 left the district.

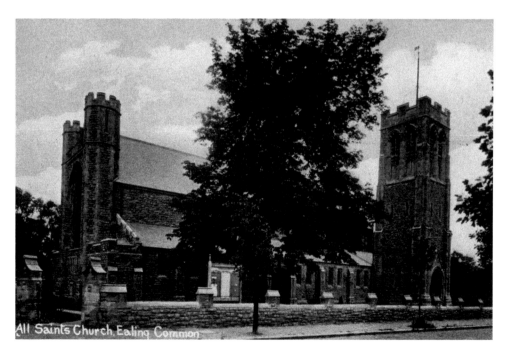

All Saints' Church, Ealing Common, *c.* 1910.

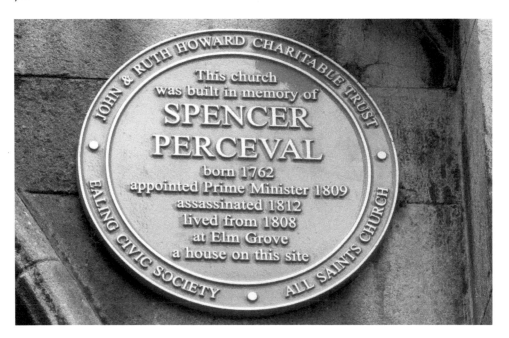

Plaque to Spencer Perceval.

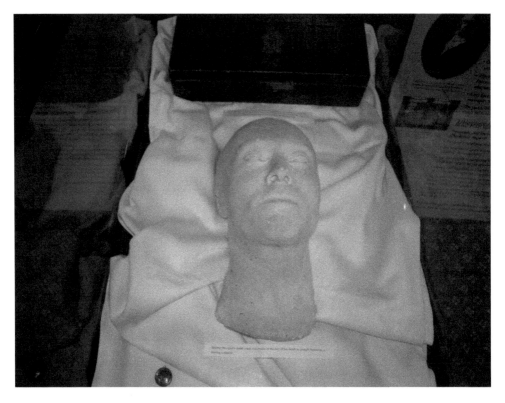

Spencer Perceval's death mask and dispatch box.

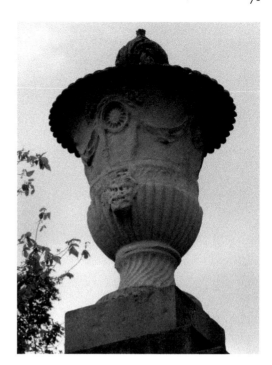

Original garden feature from Elm Grove
(former residence of Spencer Perceval).

From 1929–56 the leader of the Communist Party of Great Britain was Harry Pollitt. He had a great admiration for the Soviet Union when it was led by its most murderous despot, Joseph Stalin. He addressed an audience at Ealing Town Hall on 27 November 1935 and the audience had to pay for tickets to hear him. Two members of the Labour Party courted controversy by sharing the stage with him as their party was opposed to the Communists.

The years between the world wars saw the emergence of political extremism as a response both to and against the Bolshevik revolution in Russia in 1917 and this was reflected in this district, too. Communism was limited to isolated individuals and small groups (a group was founded in Acton in 1938 and in Hanwell in 1935), but Fascism was stronger. At first this was represented in both Ealing and Acton by units of the British Fascists. These were established in the early 1920s and they seem quite active, with regular meetings for discussions about national and international events, and with invited speakers, many being held at The Three Pigeons pub on Ealing High Street, as well as public meetings on the Common or at the Mount in Acton. Despite their Acton leader being a man called Andrew Slaughter, the group seems to have been largely peaceful and was certainly not anti-Semitic. British Fascists had policies similar to those of the orthodox Conservative Party and they do not seem to have links with Continental Fascism. They provided volunteers to help run transport services during the General Strike of 1926. However, by the late 1920s they ceased to exist.

More prevalent in Ealing and Acton, in the next decade, were the British Union of Fascists, rather different from their predecessors in being violent, anti-Semitic and with Nazi sympathies. Even these were a minority, but they were not quite wholly disreputable, being listed in local publications along with other political parties. Robert Ling was their

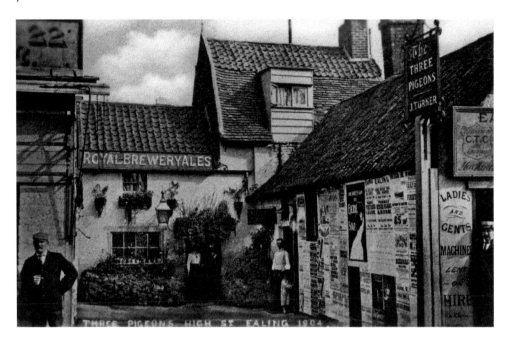

Three Pigeons public house, High Street, Ealing.

Ealing agent and Dr Claude Gouldes-Brough, their prospective parliamentary candidate in Acton. There were many letters by them and their opponents in the local press over matters such as the Spanish Civil War, and also instances of fighting during public meetings. Fascists were banned from speaking in Southall Park but the Labour council allowed their opponents, the Communist Party, to speak there.

Fascist leaders visited the locality on several occasions. Sir Oswald Mosley was known locally, having been Conservative MP for Harrow in 1918–22 and this constituency then included Greenford and Hanwell. Mosley at this time resided in Greenford. As a local MP he had been popular (constituents clubbed together to buy him and his first wife a wedding present), despite the disparity in wealth.

In the years after he had joined the Labour Party, but thwarted politically, founded his own, where he was leader. He was leader of the British Union of Fascists, anti-Semitic and an open admirer of Hitler. In the 1930s he addressed public meetings in Ealing on three occasions. The first two took place at Ealing Town Hall on 9 November 1933 and 22 July 1935 (not something that will be mentioned by those leading tours around the place) and attracted large audiences. Like Hitler he was a charismatic speaker.

However, in October 1936, with opinion hardening against his movement, which had been shown up as being violent, the (Conservative) council banned him – as well as any representative of the Communist or Fascist parties – from speaking in council property. Undeterred, flanked by his supporters, he spoke to crowds at the corner of Melbourne Avenue, West Ealing. There were opponents there, including local Jews and trade unionists, but despite the heckling there was no physical violence on either side. William Joyce was another prominent Fascist who visited Ealing and Acton and addressed the party faithful.

It is not only the leaders of extremist parties which have caused local consternation. During the 1930s Frank Sanderson, MP for the (sole) constituency of Ealing from 1931–45, made a bold suggestion in October 1938 at a Conservative Party meeting in West Ealing, about the correct attitude that should be held toward the German Chancellor, Hitler. According to him, 'If we are going to conserve the peace of the world, we must make up our minds that we are to trust those with whom we are associating... We have got to live alongside the dictatorship countries. Nothing can prevent it.' Sanderson had some sympathy with German grievances stemming from the end of the First World War: 'Since I have been your member, since 1931. And since before then, I have done all it has been possible to do to urge a revision of the Treaty of Versailles.'

The newspaper's initial reaction was complimentary: 'Seldom, if ever, has Sir Frank made in Ealing a better speech than this.' Yet their editorial summed up the speech as 'Trust Hitler' and some writing into the local newspaper were critical of his attitude. Germany had just taken part of Czechoslovakia and Britain and France had acquiesced in order to prevent a European war, and most people agreed to this appeasement. At a meeting in the next month he reiterated his point: 'Yes, I do mean trust Hitler. You must trust those with whom you are working, or you must have isolation. I am not in favour of isolation at the moment from the rest of Europe.'

Before condemning Sanderson outright, it should be recalled that Britain and Germany were then at peace and that the latter had not yet commenced their campaign of mass murder against the Jews and other peoples. Yet the new German regime had shown their clear contempt for human rights by gaoling political opponents and Jews, though not as yet killing them wholesale. Chamberlain's policy was favoured by most in Ealing as well as in England as it prevented immediate war. When the German army marched into the remainder of Czechoslovakia in March 1939, Sanderson stated that it was now no longer possible to accept Nazi guarantees. Despite his words and actions in 1938, Sanderson was re-elected as MP for Ealing in 1945, though the borough had been by now divided into two constituencies (the other voted in a Labour man).

One organisation that was established on a national basis in 1937 and founded a branch in Ealing and Acton in February 1938 was The Link. This was a movement which sought to foster better relations between Britain and Germany, recognising that the peoples of both countries desired peace. Needless to say they were very pleased with the events in 1938 but locally were not heard of once war began.

In the later twentieth century, prime ministers (including Alec Douglas-Home, Harold Wilson, and James Callaghan) gave election addresses locally; until the 1960s it was not deemed necessary for such highly exalted men to do so. Yet in 1901, a then young man, who was later to become the greatest of them all, arrived in Ealing to give a speech at Ealing Town Hall.

That man was none other than Winston Churchill. He was speaking about his recent experiences in South Africa, when as a journalist he had been captured by the Boers and then dramatically escaped. On 21 October 1901 at the behest of the Ealing Green Literary and Music Society, the aspiring statesman gave a lantern slide lecture at the Victoria Hall, in Ealing Town Hall. The journalist reporting the event wrote, 'At first one was not greatly impressed with his manner of speaking', as if it was a difficulty for him.

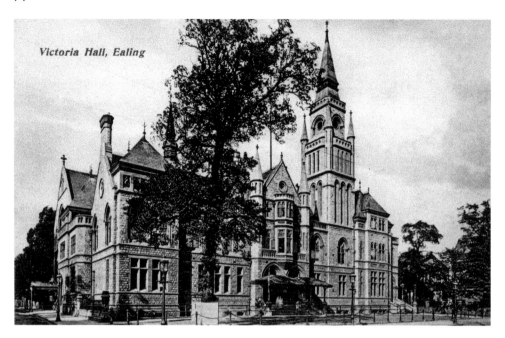

Victoria Hall (entrance at the side), Ealing.

However, in describing his escape from Boer captivity his language was noted as being 'vigorous, terse, plain and unexaggerated'. In his showing of photographs of blurry battle scenes in which everything was confused and undistinguishable, he explained, 'That is a very good view of a modern battle. You cannot make out anything.'

Political suicide is usually a term referring to a politician who makes such a major gaffe or commits such a serious offence that they are obliged to step down from politics. It is not meant to be taken literally. We have already seen that one MP took his life (see the Espionage chapter), but there was another aspiring politician in the locality who did so, too. This was Barbara Maddin, who was Conservative candidate for the Southall parliamentary constituency on two occasions in the 1960s. This has always been a Labour stronghold, but it was not the entirely impregnable safe seat that it is now.

Barbara Maddin was a barrister and a magistrate, born in 1929, with an interest in politics, having been a Richmond councillor from 1959–63. She was narrowly defeated in the Southall election in 1964 by a mere 2,000 votes and more comprehensively in 1966 by 5,300. She was Vice President of the Conservative National Women's Council and of the Southall Young Conservatives. Her particular interest was in the study of penal conditions and she lectured widely.

By 1968 she seems to have stepped down as a potential MP and resided at Vicarage Court, Vicarage Gate, Kensington. On the night of Saturday 3 February 1973, one Martin Lindman saw something in the Thames near Lower Ham Road, Kingston. He tried to rescue the woman but it was too late. This was Barbara Maddin and the inquest found that she had died from drowning. It seems that she was suffering from anxiety and depression, for her mother was unwell and she was feeling pressurised through work.

DID YOU KNOW?

Ealing houses one of the few embassies in suburban rather than central London. This is the Embassy of the Democratic People's Republic of Korea (i.e. North Korea), located at No. 73 Gunnersbury Avenue since 2003, when this seven-bedroomed house was bought for £1.3 million. In 2016 the deputy ambassador defected to South Korea and in 2017 the embassy was evacuated due to a bomb threat. The current ambassador is His Excellency Mr Choe II.

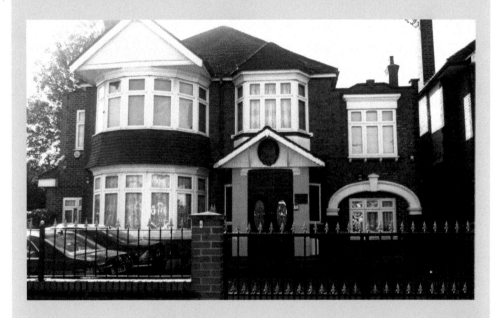

Above: North Korean Embassy, Gunnersbury Avenue.

Right: Embassy plaque, North Korean Embassy.

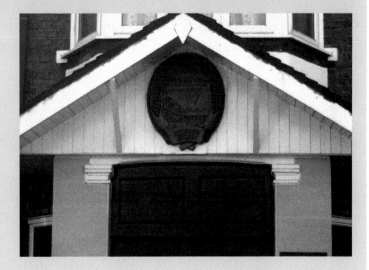

10. Scandal

It is difficult to discuss modern scandals for fear of libel, and some are too well known to be worth repetition, such as the misdemeanours of a minority of the monkish teachers at St Benedict's. However, there is a prevalence of human nature among some of those in positions of public trust in the past.

Charles Jones (1830–1913) is often hailed as the epitome of Ealing's golden age: borough surveyor and architect for 50 years, designer of the town hall and other municipal buildings, churches, schools and much of the town's Victorian infrastructure, as well as being a pillar of the Congregational church. Truly Ealing's Grand Old Man, to whom a plaque was recently unveiled on Windsor Road. He even coined the phrase in 1901 of Ealing as being 'Queen of Suburbs', one that has certainly stuck. Yet three charges can be brought against him.

The first is that he used his position on the council to feather his own nest. As surveyor and engineer he was best placed to know of the town's future development and to be able to influence the erection of infrastructure, as well as being influential in granting permission to any buildings erected in his role on the Works Committee (a de facto planning committee). However, Jones was also a property developer and had a foot in both camps. Along with Dr Ebenezer Pearce and Alfred Priest, he bought land cheaply

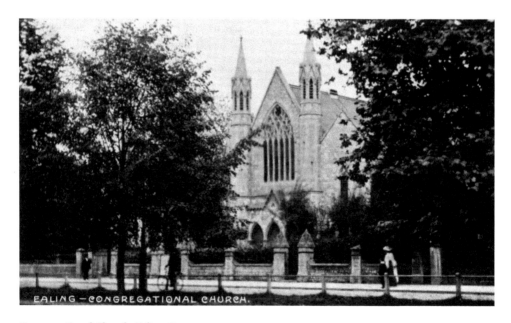

Congregational Church, Ealing Green.

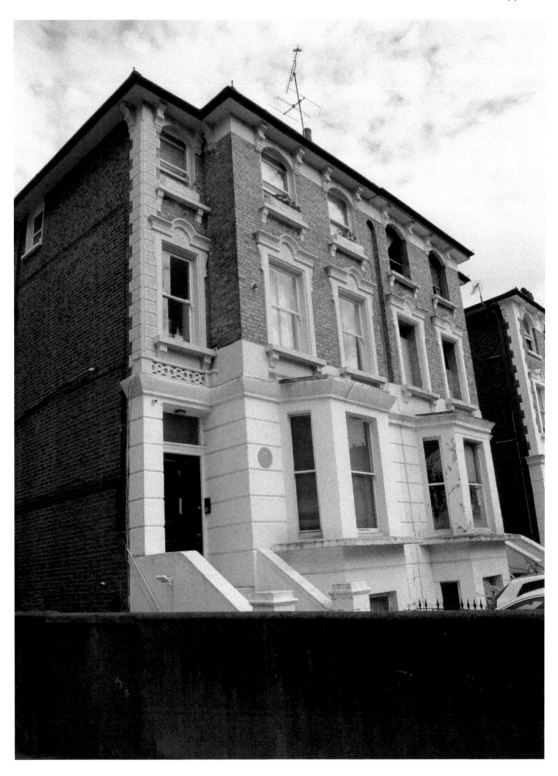

No. 5 Windsor Road, Ealing.

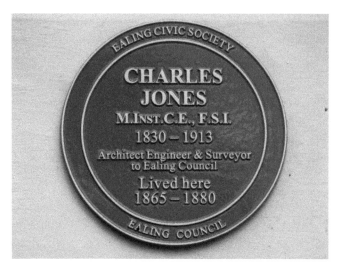

Left: Plaque to Charles Jones, Windsor Road, Ealing.

Below: Memorial to Charles Jones, Walpole Park, Ealing.

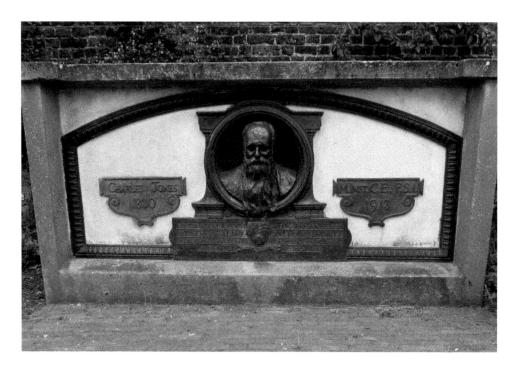

in north Ealing in July 1870 following the bankruptcy of speculator Austin de Bruno. Houses had to be of a minimum value: £700 or more if detached and £500 or more if semi-detached (there were to be no terraced houses, or places of entertainment, or shops). This meant that they could sell at a high rate to builders and the latter would know that Jones would be able to approve their development schemes without any bother as he was on the committee that gave the go-ahead (or not) to developers. There seems to have been no public outcry that Jones' knowledge and contacts might well have profited him personally and a conflict of interests certainly seems to have existed.

He was also accused of being what would be termed currently as a 'public sector fat cat'. There is a cartoon from around 1900 showing a bearded elderly man (clearly Jones but not explicitly named) with a bag of money, marked £1,000 (Jones's annual salary). A street sweeper stands nearby, and remarks, 'It's alright for you, but some of us have to get by on far less.' It was true that pay gaps between those at the top and those at the bottom were extreme. Curiously enough, Jones was paid more than the Town Clerk (£650 p.a.), the head of the council's salaried officials, and he was senior to Jones. There was criticism in other quarters, too, with Councillor Gooding pointing out that borough surveyors elsewhere were paid half of what Jones was earning, from £200–£500 a year, even where the towns in question were bigger than Ealing, such as Brighton and Hull. Furthermore, he was earning money from other commissions, such as from Hanwell Council, too. Defenders pointed out Jones' vast and unique experience of Ealing: 'His salary is now £1000, but this is a somewhat unusual salary for a Borough Surveyor and it is due to his great length of service, and there is a good deal of knowledge he has acquired during the course of it which is a considerable saving of expense to the corporation in other ways.'

It should also be noted that he was a surveyor; he never had any architectural qualifications or experience, but was the mastermind behind the design of numerous buildings in the district. None of this was alluded to when the eulogies for Jones came on his death in 1913.

A rogue official was Hanwell's third librarian, Frank Stinton, appointed in 1920. He suffered from ill health (and so avoided a combatant role in the First World War). He died

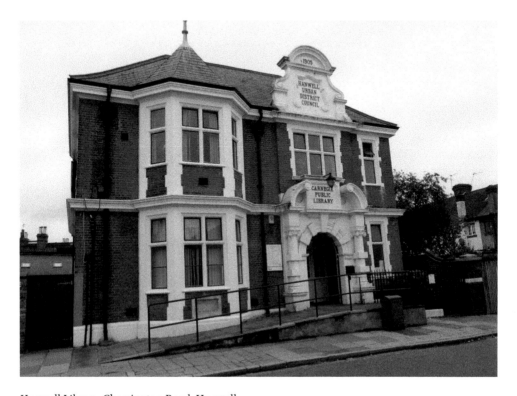

Hanwell Library, Cherrington Road, Hanwell.

in December 1923 and the library committee's instant response was 'that a letter of sympathy and condolence be forwarded to his widow'. However, it was soon found, after an examination of the library's account books, that they had to 'regret to report that upon the death of the librarian it was found that cash taken in the library in the month of November, which the librarian should have paid to the treasurer at the beginning of December, had not been paid in'. The sum of £33 10s 4d was missing. It was later found that 'deficiencies in the accounts relating to the hire of rooms, in which sum amounting to £6 7s 6d for which receipts had been issued and the counterfeits fraudulently altered by the late librarian'. The grieving widow was then called in for an interview as to where it was, but she had no idea. It is not known what Stinton did with it, but presumably he spent it on gambling, drink or women.

There have also been a number of clergy – a minority, it is true – whose behaviour was less than what it should have been, involving themselves in scandal and controversy. Seventeenth-century clergy were often caught up with the tumultuous events of the Civil Wars; Acton's rector had to flee soldiers and the Ealing vicar was ousted, as was his Greenford counterpart. Northolt's rector was even accused of unnatural relations with his sister. Dr William Dodd, a clergyman who ran a school in Ealing in the following century, was hanged for forging a money bond.

The Revd William Lambert was the first man appointed as curate to the newly built Christ Church in Ealing in 1852. He was an elderly Irishman. However, he came to the attention of the diocesan authorities on two scandalous topics. First of all he attended a séance in a house on Ealing Green with a notorious medium, and Lambert later claimed that he saw objects moving. Anglican clergy were not meant to attend such events, nor to endorse the manifestations allegedly witnessed there. Secondly, he was accused of having made a young female parishioner pregnant. This was less certain. However, he was hauled before the Church's diocesan consistory court in 1856 and was suspended from his living for four years.

An Anglican curate in Acton, the American-born Revd Turbenille Cory-Thomas, at St Albans' from 1898, claimed to take his responsibilities outside the church very seriously. One of his female parishioners (never named in public) needed to discuss matters with him in private. He arranged a meeting with her in a hotel in central London and they met in a private room there. He also saw her in her own house, too. His vicar received information suggesting that improper relations took place between the curate and the woman. The woman claimed that Cory-Thomas had embraced her and kissed her and apparently later asked her to be his mistress. Naturally he denied all this and took his employer, the Revd Bernard Spink, to court for defamation of character. The court found against Cory-Thomas and he never worked for the Church of England again. Whether he was guilty or not, he was at the very least very foolish.

Mr Henry Bisoce, Greenford rector from 1891, ran into money troubles and used his position to try and rectify his situation. As rector he was in charge of various funds set aside for charitable purposes. In 1895 another trustee, Mr Perkin, asked him about these monies and Biscoe told him that they were with the Charity Commissioners. On enquiry by Perkin, this was found to be untrue, so he tasked Biscoe again with the matter. He then claimed he had deposited them at the Bank of England, and once again Perkin uncovered another untruth.

The case was then brought into the open at Brentford Magistrates' Court and then at the Old Bailey. It appeared that Biscoe was in debt to the tune of £2,500 and had an annual income of about £350. As a childless bachelor this should have been enough to live on. He had taken other measures to stave off creditors and had used money from school and other charity accounts, including cash meant for poor parishioners at Christmastime. Bisoce made no further attempt to deny the charges and his defence urged leniency, which was granted. Bisoce left Greenford but remained rector and died in 1918. It is presumed that he aspired to a lifestyle to which he could not afford and became indebted to an impossible degree.

Hanwell's Catholic priest in the 1930s was Monseigneur Henry Barton Brown. He became a figure of hate for some in 1937 when he commented in public about the ongoing Spanish Civil War. He saw it as a struggle between the Catholic Church and the atheistic Communists. He told his congregation that if he was Spanish he would take up arms against the left-wing government, who had adopted an anti-Catholic stance. Anyone who supported the Spanish government, as many in the British Labour Party did, should not receive one vote from a Catholic voter. His critics seized upon his first statement to suggest that the priest was advocating armed insurrection and was a man of violence despite his sacred profession. They called for him to be dropped from the council's education committee for such views.

Another 'turbulent' priest was Father Richard O'Halloran, who was Ealing's first post-reformation Catholic priest and his church, the Mission of St Joseph and St Peter, was on Mattock Lane from at least 1893. He came into conflict with his church authorities in the form of Cardinal Vaughan in 1899 when a parish was established centred at St Benedict's. O'Halloran would not obey the diocese and was suspended, and then excommunicated in 1914. O'Halloran's attacks on the church hierarchy, though not towards the Pope, also did not enamour him to his superiors. Yet he retained his loyal congregation and carried on being priest until his death in 1925. However, it should be recalled that most officials, both secular and spiritual, have carried out their duties without any smear on their reputations.

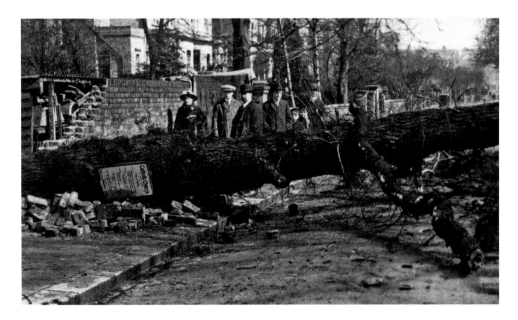

Catholic Church notice on tree uprooted in gale, 1916, Mattock Lane, Ealing.

11. Sport

Ealing is not usually viewed as being one of the most famous sporting districts in London; it has no Wimbledon nor Twickenham and the nearest league football club is Brentford. Yet in the past there were a number of sports for which the locality was famous: hunting, shooting, racing and tennis. The latter is still played locally, but most of the others are now long defunct.

The rural nature of the district led it to be used for hunts. The Royal Buck hunt met at Northolt in the 1880s to hunt a stag especially released for the purpose. Mr A. W. Perkins seems to have instituted drag hunts from Greenford to Northolt from 1888 at least and they were still taking place in the early 1900s. This was replaced by the Middlesex Farmers' Drag Hunt once Perkin became too ill to continue. This continued until at least the 1930s with the Pinner Farmers' Drag Hunt.

Frederick Crees, a Northolt farmer, was enthusiastic about hunting, which he took a part in: 'The drag itself was made up of aniseed and several other smelly confections, all put in a bag and dragged by a runner at the end of a length of rope. He started an hour before the hunt began running about three miles across country, then there was a check. Some riders changed horses and some rode the same all the time. Then there was another three miles of drag, a check and then home again, where the runner would have a quantity of meat ready for the hounds to tear to pieces. The Master would be blowing his horn and the whipper in "Tally ho-ing."'

Ealing's horse-racing history goes back to the early nineteenth century. The Ealing Races were held in Dean Gardens, West Ealing. There were two races, each for prizes of £50. A poster shows one for 1819, but cannot have lasted beyond 1832, because the land was passed over from the bishop of London as allotments.

Greenford and Northolt boasted racing grounds in the 1920s and 1930s, just as these districts became built up. In Greenford, from 7 July 1919 there were the 'trotting tracks' where two ponies were affixed to a small two-wheeled cart with a jockey and raced around the tracks. People came from London to participate, to watch and to gamble. In Anthony Powell's novel *The Acceptance World*, he has an Italian restauranteur, Foppa, as a regular attender: 'He was a great gambler, and sometimes spent his weekends taking part in trotting races somewhere not far from London, perhaps at Greenford in Middlesex.'

The track was just off Birkbeck Avenue and was run by the London Trotting Club. Greenford was presumably chosen because it was close to London and easily accessible by both train and car. Professionals and amateurs entered the races. Gates opened at 12 noon and the first race was at 2.10 p.m. Apparently it had the widest cinder track in the country. However, it was frequented by criminal gangs who levied protection money on the bookies. The track became used for greyhound racing and motorbike contests by the 1930s and closed a few years later, to be built over for housing.

Further to the west, another racing venue was being established. From 1928–29 the Northolt racecourse – where horses, not ponies raced – was built at, allegedly, the cost of a quarter of a million pounds. The Earl of Harewood opened it in 1929. It was extended in 1936 and was famous for its stands and its refreshment pavilion. It was used in the George Formby film *Come on George* in 1939.

The year 1939 spelt an end to the racecourse. It was converted for military use during the war, first as an ordnance depot and then as a place to hold Italian prisoners of war. It was not reopened after 1945 despite efforts to do so and the land was purchased in 1951; complete demolition occurred in 1955 and the only reminder of its existence is that one of the original gates survives, and that local roads were named after racing venues such as Ascot and Newmarket.

Shooting ranges were also in evidence to the north of our district, notably in Perivale, from at least 1865. It was to the west of Perivale Lane and the north of the Brent and to what is now south of the Western Avenue. Initially it was a rifle range and was used by the rifle associations and various militia forces of Middlesex, the former established at this time for fear of a French invasion.

On 31 August 1886 when militiamen were expending 7,000 rounds of ammunition, smoke was seen from the iron shed which housed over 50,000 cartridges. Attempts were made with water to douse the flames, but to no effect and so all present stood well back, awaiting the inevitable explosion. When it came, no one was hurt, but the bang was heard as far away as south Ealing. Police and firemen came to the site but there was no obvious cause.

However, from around 1900, amid the farmers' fields, it was reinvented as the West London Shooting Grounds, of around 100 acres, which provided lessons as well as guns

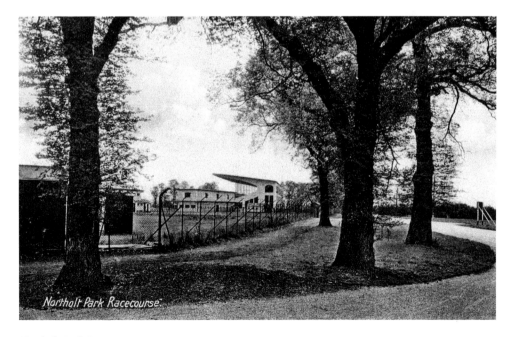

Northolt Park Racecourse.

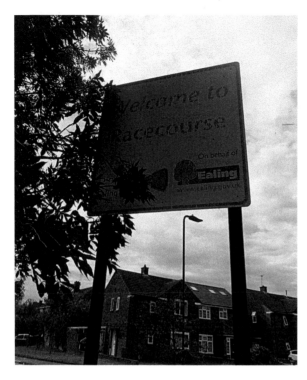

Left: Sign to the Racecourse (Council) Estate.

Below: Site of the former racecourse, Northolt.

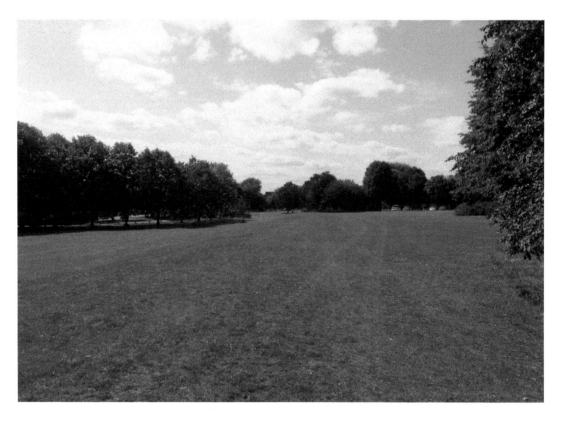

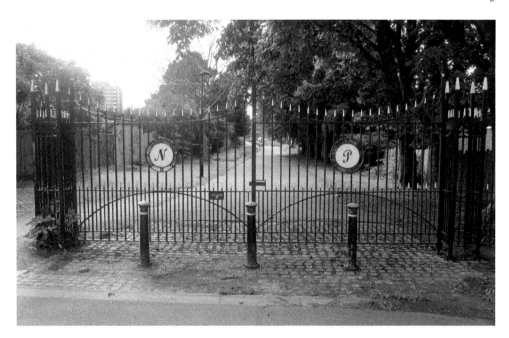

Northolt Park Racecourse gates.

and ammunition – apparently they boasted the world's record heap of used cartridges. Initially it was developed so that sportsmen could practise before the grouse and pheasant shooting season in August. Those who patronised this site included Lords Balfour and Lovat. What was shot here were not live targets but clay pigeons, and there were specially built (by Charles Jones) grouse and partridge lodges and butts. The school moved from Perivale to Northolt in 1931 to make way for the construction of the Hoover Building, so perhaps modified, the school claims to be the oldest in the country.

Although Fred Perry's association with Ealing in the 1920s and 1930s is very well known, he was not the only Ealing tennis star, just the most 'recent' one. In fact, there were a number of female tennis players in the late nineteenth and early twentieth centuries. Only one of these has been locally acknowledged. This is Dorothea Chambers, née Douglas. Born in 1878, she was the daughter of the vicar of St Matthew's Church in Ealing and attended the now defunct Princess Helena College in north Ealing. She recalled learning tennis by playing in the vicarage gardens and later played at school where she clashed with the games mistress over the rules. She also played at the Ealing Lawn Tennis Club, joining as a junior in 1889 and often played with men as well as with women.

She won the club's singles' competition in 1899 and the ladies' singles in 1901. Her Wimbledon debut was in 1900. She won the ladies' singles there in 1903, 1904, 1906, 1910, 1911, 1913 and 1914. She also played in the ladies' doubles finals in 1913, 1919 and 1920, but not successfully. In 1908 she won the gold medal for tennis at the Olympics. In later life she was a coach and also played hockey and badminton.

There were another three female ace tennis players associated with Ealing in the late Victorian era. Charlotte Cooper, born in Ealing in 1870, was one. At an early age she joined

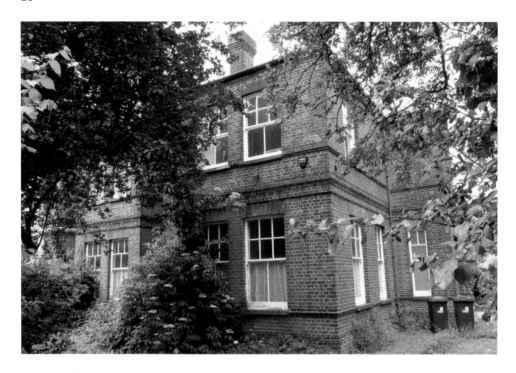

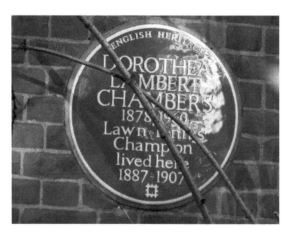

Above: Former house of Dorothea Lambert Chambers, North Common Road, Ealing.

Left: Plaque to Dorothea Lambert Chambers.

Ealing Lawn Tennis Club and went on to win the ladies' Singles at Wimbledon in 1895, 1896, 1898, 1901 and 1908. In 1904 she played Dorothea Douglas and lost in the finals. She also won the gold medal at the Olympics in tennis in 1900.

Blanche Bingley was born in Greenford in 1863 and lived with her family in Stanhope Park, a mansion standing in large grounds. She won the 'ladies' singles at Wimbledon in 1886, 1889, 1894, 1897, 1899 and 1900.

Finally there was Mary Sutton, who was born in 1886 and lived in Acton as a small child, but later moved to the USA. She was victorious at the ladies' singles at Wimbledon in 1905 and 1907, beating Dorothea Chambers, but losing against her in 1906.

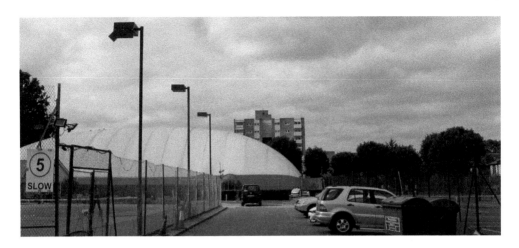

Ealing Lawn Tennis Club, Daniel Road, Ealing.

DID YOU KNOW?

Ealing is not known for its football as some other districts in London are. There were, however, numerous amateur teams. One of these was the short-lived Southall Wanderers, which appears to have been in existence for only four seasons, from 1935/1936 to 1938/1939. As with some other local teams they played in the Dauntless League and were in the second and third divisions of this amateur league. There seems to have been goals aplenty in the matches they played; in a match in December 1936 they scored 10-2 against the Marylebone Presbyterian team, but in 1938 they lost by 12 goals to 2 against Clifton Road Old Boys. Presumably the outbreak of war in September 1939 and the call-up of most of the players put a stop to the club. Ironically in 1931 there had been a Southall Wanderers Cricket team, though this was even shorter lived.

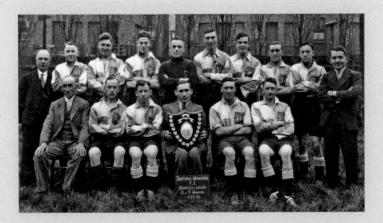

Southall Wanderers Football Club.

12. Vanished Buildings

The countryside which is now the London Borough of Ealing once contained numerous stately homes and rambling rectories in or near the villages just a few miles from the capital. As time has passed and population has risen, many of these properties have been sold, demolished and their grounds built on, especially in the boom of the early twentieth century. A few survive – Pitzhanger Manor, Norwood Hall, Rochester House, Gunnersbury Park, Greenford Hall and Greenford Rectory – but most do not. So what then, has been lost of the past?

Certainly anyone only knowing the borough as it has existed for the past few decades might struggle with the fact that for most of its history Ealing was a collection of villages, with mansions, cottages and rectories. One relatively recent loss was Berrymede Priory, which was confusingly not built as a religious building and was only briefly in the mid-nineteenth century used for ecclesiastical purposes. It was a mansion standing in substantial grounds to the south of Acton High Street. It was built in around 1802 in the Gothic style then popular (Twyford Abbey nearby is a surviving example of the type).

For much of the nineteenth century it was a private family home. In 1885 it was bought by the Acton Constitutional Club as their headquarters, whilst most of the land was sold

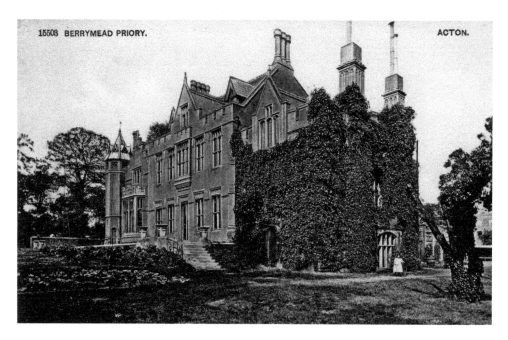

Berrymede Priory, Acton.

for housing. However, in 1939 it was sold again, this time to Neville's Bakeries to use as offices. In 1977 they left as the place began to fall into a derelict state. Despite a Grade II listed status, the council gave permission to have it destroyed and this took place in 1984. The site is now partly a car park and partly housing, recalled only by street names.

Another listed building whose listed status proved an ineffectual defence was Perivale Rectory. This stood to the north of the ancient church of St Mary the Virgin in Perivale, and was home for centuries to the rector. In the early twentieth century it was noted as being partly made of medieval materials whilst ostensibly outwardly appearing to be archetypal Tudor. It often appeared on postcards and in borough guides showing both church and rectory as picturesque medieval survivals in the modern (1930s/50s) age.

The difficulty was that it was expensive to maintain, as all old buildings are. If the rector was a man of wealth, this was not an insolvable issue, but if not, then an increasingly cash-strapped Church of England was reluctant to pay for what it saw as a mere historic monument. The twentieth century was not a sentimental age as far as rectories were concerned (those in Acton, Northolt and Hanwell were demolished; that in Norwood fell victim to enemy action). Repairs were needed in the early 1950s for it to be habitable and these were expensive and could be ongoing.

Some urged that the building should be preserved as a museum or as offices. John Petingale, a Greenford antiquarian, and John Betjeman, the poet and conservationist, were two such protesters. However, their pleas fell on deaf ears. In 1958 the building's listed status was removed and by the following year it was no more.

Suffolk House was once one of the Acton's landmarks until its demolition in 1963. It was one of a pair of detached large brick-made houses, known collectively as the Siamese Twins, the other being Lichfield House. They were both built in the middle of the eighteenth century for Thomas Mandeville and stood on the north side of the High

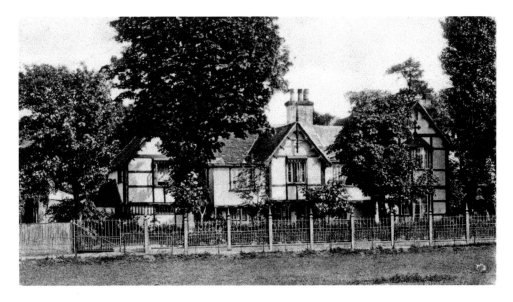

Perivale Rectory.

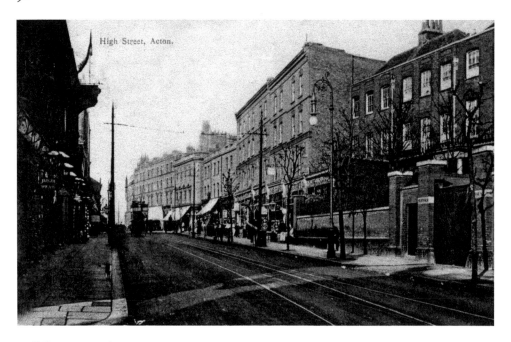

Suffolk House, High Street, Acton.

Street, opposite Oldham Terrace. Shops were built in front of them in the early twentieth century and they increasingly became white elephants.

Built in part of the former grounds of Suffolk House was the Globe Cinema, which was Acton's third cinema and which opened in 1921. It was designed by Mr G. Perry Pratt and built by the Ferris Brothers, all of whom were Acton men. It was briefly the largest cinema outside America and it took its name from a rotating globe at the top of the building, which was lit up at night time. In 1949 it became a Gaumont cinema and closed in 1959 before being demolished in 1966 for shops to be built on the site.

There were two buildings in Hanwell which fell to the developer in the years before the First World War. One was the Lawns. It stood just to the north of the Uxbridge Road and its grounds went as far north as the railway line. It had been home from 1841–66 to reforming mental health surgeon Dr John Conolly (1794–1866), who had been superintendent and later Visiting Physician to the nearby County Asylum. He went into private practice here.

However, by the first decade of the twentieth century no one individual or family wished to live here. It was broken down into flats, lived in by less affluent people. Eventually, shortly after 1901 it was demolished and housing now covers the site. The only remnant is the small park known as Conolly Dell, which represented the north of the grounds, which was opened in 1909.

Hanwell's only mansion proper was Hanwell Park, dating to the seventeenth century, which stood in its own grounds, which at their furthest extent were of 300 acres in 1767. It stood to the east of what is now Greenford Avenue and extended eastwards to the parish boundary with Ealing, to the south of the Uxbridge Road and to the north with the Brent. It was rebuilt by John Nash in the early nineteenth century and was Grecian

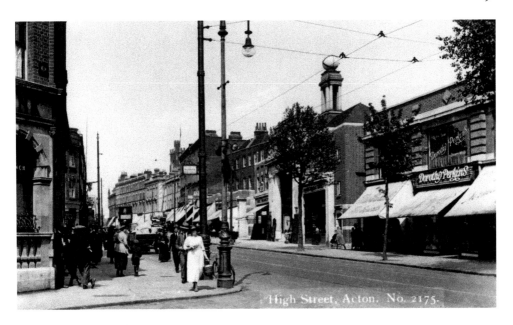

The Globe cinema, High Street, Acton.

in appearance, 'a very favourable specimen of Grecian architecture', with a central block, two wings and Doric pillars. There were two walled gardens to its east, fine elms and oaks.

As the nineteenth century progressed, owners sold land off for building, 106 acres being sold in 1883 and another 48 ten years later. The last owner was Commander Benjamin Sharpe, from 1848–83, and his son then sold the place. There was talk of it being used by the Hanwell School Board, and then more realistic discussion in 1901 about its use as a hotel, with an additional forty bedrooms being built on. Neither of these plans came to anything and so after some years of its standing derelict, it was demolished.

Fordhook was an Ealing house which had associations with three famous names. It was built in the seventeenth century just off the north of what is now the Uxbridge Road and not far from the Common. In 1753 it was the home of famous playwright, novelist and magistrate Henry Fielding (1708–54). Having lived in London for years, country-born Fielding was finding that it was bad for his health. He lived at Fordhook for a few months, but finding his health no better took ship to Lisbon where he died.

The house's literary associations did not end there. Lady Noel Byron, widow of the poet, lived in Ealing for many years and from 1832–40 resided at Fordhook. Whilst here she put her educational theories into practice and founded a school on Ealing Green in 1834. It was also at Fordhook that her only child, Ada, was married to Lord Lovelace and Ada worked with Charles Babbage in the development of ideas that in the next century resulted in the invention of the computer.

Many others lived at Fordhook, but at the beginning of the twentieth century with housing development mushrooming locally, the house was sold and demolished in 1903. It is now remembered by the street names Fordhook Avenue and Fielding Crescent, just opposite the Ealing Common tube station.

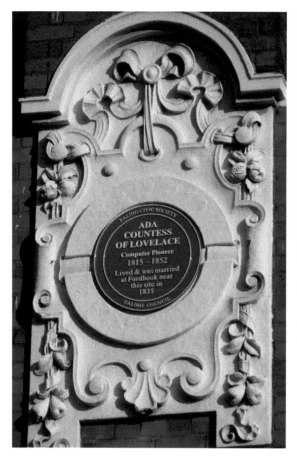

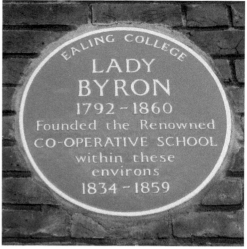

Above: Plaque to Lady Byron, University of West London.

Left: Plaque to Ada, Countess of Lovelace, Fordhook Avenue, Ealing.

Chignell House was on the north side of the Uxbridge Road in West Ealing. In the nineteenth century its site was marked by a memorial on a building on its site, not far from the Old Hat pub. It was a school run by the Chignell sisters from at least 1832 to 1839, with Mary Chignell running it as a boarding school for eight girls, aged eight to fifteen by 1840. Revd and Mrs Hickson continued to run it as a school later in the century but by 1881 it ceased functioning as a school and was demolished by 1886, being replaced by a set of houses known as Chignell Terrace.

In 1871 a house at the top of Northfields Lane was leased to be run as a cottage hospital, the first in the district. Funds were raised to pay a matron, a nurse and a cook and two doctors agreed to provide their part-time services for free. Over the next few years, the house was extended in 1873, its freehold purchased in 1886 and hundreds of patients were taken as inpatients (in the past they had to go to London for treatment). In 1871 there were only three beds and twenty-seven inpatients; by 1901 there were twenty-two and 216 in 1901; in thirty years there had been 3,471 inpatients. Jones wrote, 'Surely the work is good works and worthy of our sympathy and support.' In 1911, however, it was demolished and a cinema stood on its site. A new hospital opened on Mattock Lane, the King Edward Memorial Hospital.

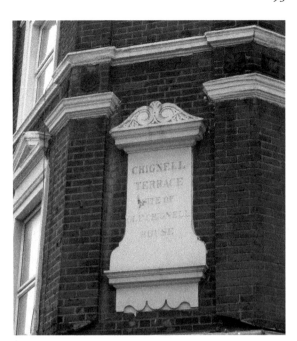

Right: Chignell House plaque,
West Ealing.

Below: Cottage Hospital,
Northfield Avenue, West Ealing.

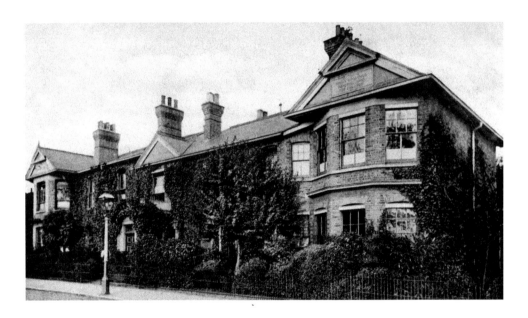

A picturesque building in Acton was the East Acton Forge, on the south side of East Acton Lane. Given the number of horses passing through and in the district in the nineteenth century, this was a lucrative proposition. This forge dated from around 1807 and Richard Atlee was an early smith there (1839). However, by 1909, the increasing use of electrical and steam power meant that passing horses were few in number and it was in that year that it stood deserted. The last smith was George Spencer. Apparently,

'To mark the unique circumstance some sentimentalists (or was it a local wag!) has planted a black flag over the chimney pot of the smithy.' It had been demolished by 1911.

Another vanished building is the St Marylebone Parochial School, which was on the west side of South Road in Southall from 1858. It was a boarding school for poor children from the parish which bore its title and was designed for a maximum of 390 children. As with the more famous Cuckoo School in Hanwell, land for building was cheaper in the countryside and, it was thought, healthier. The school closed in 1915 and was used as an Australian military hospital from 1915–18. Afterwards it reverted to being a school, St Joseph's, for Catholic girls, run by the Daughters of the Cross nuns. It closed in 1931 and was demolished for housing.

The number of pubs locally has risen and fallen over the years. The Three Pigeons on the east side of the bottom end of Ealing High Street was one. It was established in around 1851 with Joseph Blagrave as the first landlord. In the 1920s the pub hosted gatherings of the (non-anti-Semitic) Ealing Fascist Party. In the later twentieth century it changed its name to Park View and then became a restaurant, closing in 2010. (For an image of the Three Pigeons please see the chapter on Politics.)

We should not forget, however, that many vanished buildings do not require mourning. Brent Cottages, which stood along what is now the Ruislip Road in Greenford until the early twentieth century, were repeatedly condemned as being insanitary and unfit for human habitation. Similarly there were cottages in Steven's Town in West Ealing and in parts of south Acton and The Steyne, which were built cheaply and had long shelf lives. These were small houses, built as terraces and were multi-occupied.

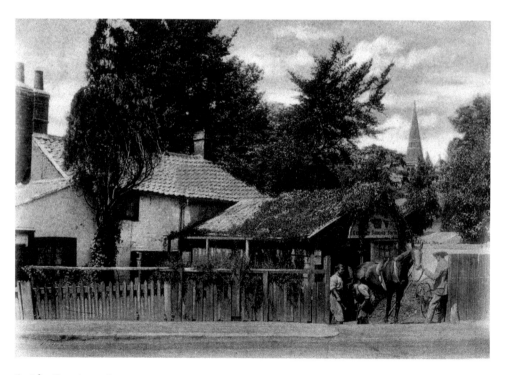

Smithy, East Acton Lane.

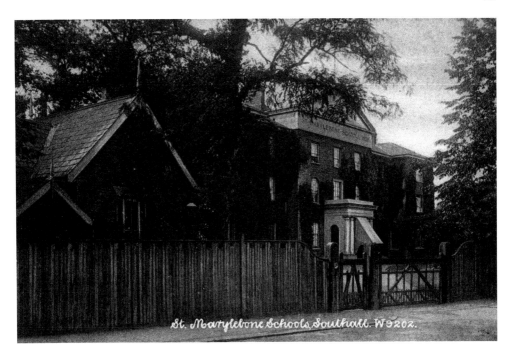

St Marylebone School, South Road, Southall.

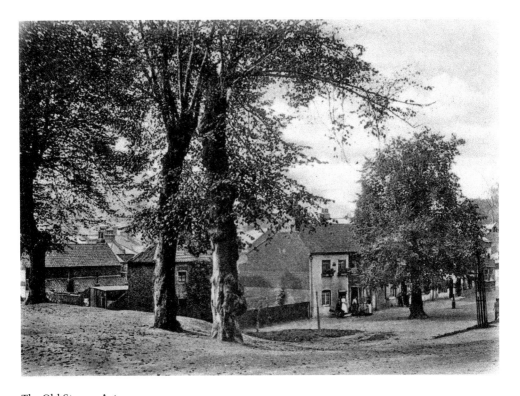

The Old Steyne, Acton.

Acknowledgements

Jean Barclay, church administrator, St Mary's Church, Ealing.

Charles Jobson and Tasmin Lang for help with photographs.

Dr Hugh Mather, St Mary's Church, Perivale.

Julia Tubman, Amy Dobson and Faustina Yawson, Gunnersbury Park Museum.

Special thanks to Colin Harris for proofreading and supplying photographs of the two Russian airmen.